"It's time to advance from success to significance. Your life can be a 'living legacy.' Greg and Ron will be your guide and this book is your manual to a life of purpose, valuable contribution and soulful reward—a life you can be proud of."

—DARREN HARDY, Publisher & Founding Editor of *SUCCESS* Magazine and *New York Times* bestselling author of *The Compound Effect.*

"Ron and Greg have managed to write a book about money that is both thought provoking and pragmatic. In You Can Do More That Matters, *they have laid out a path for thinking about the purpose of money that is inspirational as well as specific. The book weaves in useful examples of people who have harnessed the power of money to bring about good for their families and communities. This book will be helpful to anyone that is trying to balance the specific aspects of saving for education, providing for family, planning for retirement and thinking about a bigger purpose of wealth—stewardship."*

—LAWRENCE J. RYBKA, JD, CFP˚, President of ValMark Securities

"If your wealth is more than your money—and you want your money and your life to matter more—Greg and Ron's concise and enjoyable new book is just what the doctor ordered. It will not only inspire you… it will provide you with practical steps to live a more abundant life and leave a more abundant legacy. You, your family and your causes will profit."

—SCOTT KEFFER, international speaker, author, coach; CEO, Scott Keffer International

"In **You Can Do More That Matters,** *Ron and Greg challenge us to realize that the same entrepreneurial vision that creates wealth can be employed to create a legacy that exceeds all of our dreams and can make a difference in our world. They offer a way to restore power to money!"*

—**DENNIS BARIL,** Senior Pastor, Community Covenant Church, Rehoboth, MA, President, Genesis Industries Limited, L3C, Burlington, VT (a social venture company seeking to create sustainable change to systemic poverty through agribusiness product exports)

"I know personally what a book like this can do in a person's life and hope that many, many people will be impacted by reading it, become smart financial stewards, and experience the satisfaction that comes from creating wealth and giving it away for Kingdom purposes."

—**GARY SCHWAMMLEIN,** President, Willow Creek Association

"In this comprehensive treatise, the authors succinctly and compellingly illustrate the challenges and opportunities that confront successful people. More importantly, they show how we can all make our world more abundant through intelligent, in-depth planning. They show how the discernment process of our own core values allows each of us to identify the path to enriching our own lives as well as countless others. This book is a must read for all of us who wish to be fulfilled through our own positive influence and action."

—**THOMAS BRADY,** Chairman, Thomas Brady and Associates

"An engaging read from beginning to end, this book will challenge you to re-think the purpose of your money and the purpose of your life."

—**ANDREW ACCARDY,** Executive Director, Y God Institute; former Executive Vice President, Purpose Driven Ministries

"Ron and Greg tell us that, 'True wealth involves the things that money can't buy and death can't take away. Just as it is important to carefully plan how to pass on your financial wealth, we must carefully consider how we wish to pass on our true wealth to future generations.' In You Can Do More that Matters, *they make a powerful case for taking a closer look at the resources each of us is blessed to steward—and then wisely using those resources to support the causes and issues we are most passionate about. From our experience at NCF we know that those who are well-planned give more and give more wisely and experience greater joy because of it. This encouraging and useful book will inspire readers. Read it with family and friends and then plan to make a difference in your world!"*

—DAVID WILLS, President, National Christian Foundation

"Engaging and heart-felt, this book illustrates how advisors and trusted wealth consultants who have a strong personal understanding of their clients are uniquely positioned to positively impact the individuals and families they serve, and society at large."

—WADE WILKINSON, President & CEO, Securities Service Network, Inc.

YOU CAN DO
MORE
that MATTERS

YOU CAN DO
MORE
that MATTERS

If you knew you could, wouldn't you?

GREG HAMMOND, CFP®, CPA **& RON WARE,** J.D.

Wealth Impact Strategists and Personal Legacy Advisors

Published by Advantage, Charleston, South Carolina.
Member of Advantage Media Group.

ADVANTAGE is a registered trademark and the Advantage colophon is a trademark of Advantage Media Group, Inc.

Printed in the United States of America.

ISBN: 978-159932-342-8
LCCN: 2013912169

This publication is designed to provide accurate and authoritative information in regard to the subject matter covered. It is sold with the understanding that the publisher is not engaged in rendering legal, accounting, or other professional services. If legal advice or other expert assistance is required, the services of a competent professional person should be sought.

Advantage Media Group is proud to be a part of the Tree Neutral® program. Tree Neutral offsets the number of trees consumed in the production and printing of this book by taking proactive steps such as planting trees in direct proportion to the number of trees used to print books. To learn more about Tree Neutral, please visit **www.treeneutral.com**. To learn more about Advantage's commitment to being a responsible steward of the environment, please visit **www.advantagefamily.com/green**

Advantage Media Group is a publisher of business, self-improvement, and professional development books and online learning. We help entrepreneurs, business leaders, and professionals share their Stories, Passion, and Knowledge to help others Learn & Grow. Do you have a manuscript or book idea that you would like us to consider for publishing? Please visit **advantagefamily.com** or call **1.866.775.1696**.

Dedications

Greg Hammond:
To my wife, Karen, whose love and support empowers me to do more that matters, and my amazing daughters, Kelsey and Lindsey, who are my "why."

Ron Ware:
To my inspiration to create my own impactful life and legacy: God's perfect gift for me, my wife, Cheryl, and three of my brightest lights in this world, my children Andrew, Rachel, and Brenna.

. . . .

Also, to the loyal clients whom it has been our privilege to serve over the years: We appreciate your trust in us and celebrate the many inspiring ways you have done more that matters. And to our readers: We hope that our message will encourage you to discover and create your unique legacy.

Acknowledgments

WE WOULD LIKE TO THANK several people for their support, contributions, and guidance in writing this book.

To our business partners, Scott Iles and Josh Procaccini, and our fantastic teams at Hammond Iles Wealth Advisors and Wealth Impact Partners. They are tremendous people whose efforts do more that matters through the difference they make in the lives of our clients. We would especially like to thank Kelly Ashton Bradley and Pat Slonina Vieira for their valuable insights and assistance throughout the process of writing this book.

Thanks to everyone at Advantage Media and our editor, Bob Sheasley, for their assistance in bringing our passion and message to life.

To Scott Keffer, our friend, colleague, and coach, for his guidance, continued support, and inspiration. We also greatly appreciate his contributions to our knowledge and businesses and for the use of his Finishing Strong diagram in our businesses and this book.

Thanks to The Legacy Companies, LLC, for permission to use the Planning Pyramid and for the work they do to empower other advisors to plan with legacy in mind. We also appreciate Jay Steenhuysen and Philanthropy Coach for their tools, resources, and training.

To Andy Andrews, whose books, presentations, and fluttering butterfly wings have inspired us in our efforts to do more that matters.

To Richard Del Maestro, our new friend, audio director, coach, and engineer, whose input and coaching has brought our text to life.

Finally, to Darren Hardy, for his wisdom, guidance, and support in helping our message reach a bigger audience and make a greater impact.

Contents

*"Alas for those that never sing, but die
with all their music in them!"*

—OLIVER WENDELL HOLMES, American physician, poet, author, 1809–1894

Introduction

AN ABUNDANT
LIFE AND LEGACY

Oseola McCarty was a washerwoman with a heart. She grew up in southern Mississippi and never finished school—in sixth grade, she quit so she could take care of an ailing aunt. Her home in Hattiesburg was humble, and she made a meager living. She never married or had children, and she walked wherever she needed to go, often pushing a cart a mile to get groceries. But before she passed away in 1999 at the age of 91, she donated $150,000 to the University of Southern Mississippi.

The money that Oseola had saved so diligently, dollar by dollar, went into a trust fund designated to provide scholarships for deserving students who otherwise would not be able to go to college. She wanted to create an opportunity for others to obtain the education that she was never able to get. Her example inspired both the University of Southern Mississippi and Harvard University to award her honorary degrees.

Such was the legacy of this unpretentious woman who became Dr. Oseola McCarty, philanthropist. Throughout her life she saw a greater purpose, and though she struggled, she strived to attain it. She also left a legacy gift to her church, while also providing resources to help support her niece and nephew. All of her wealth came from what she had earned by cleaning other people's clothes—work she continued to do until arthritis forced her to stop just a few years before her death.

The charitable spirit is a relative concept. Our gifts are not measured by what others give, but by the intent in our heart. Oseola McCarty ultimately gave away 80 percent of what she had earned and saved to benefit others in ways she believed were life-changing and important. "If you want to be proud of yourself," she explained, "you have got to do things you can be proud of."

Others might give far greater sums—but perhaps a far smaller percentage of what they have. Oseola's example recalls the Bible story of the widow and her "mite." She too, gave abundantly from the little she had.

It is a lesson for all of us: Even if we think our resources are limited, we may still be able to help others more than we realize. With a generous spirit, we can make a difference. And if we have been entrusted with much to steward, grow, and protect, we may be able to leverage those resources in ways we didn't expect. We can maximize our influence on generations to come, without sacrificing our own lifetime goals and objectives.

Release the music inside you

That's the "live more, give more" spirit and attitude that we hope to inspire with this book. We hope to encourage you to think differently about your money and your passion. We want to motivate you to personally assess what you are really capable of doing and address the concerns and needs that move you. As you discover what you are actually able to do, we are confident that you will feel inspired to take action.

By taking action, we mean more than writing a check. We mean more than charitable giving and philanthropy. Our goal is to get you more engaged in making a bigger and better impact on the people, causes, and organizations you care about most. In short, we hope to help you to live more and give more.

We are part of a sleeping giant in this country and globally—and that giant is our excess financial capacity that gives us the potential to improve the lives of others. The vast majority of us don't truly understand what we can contribute, financially and otherwise, to the causes that matter to us. As a result, if we fail to take action, we risk becoming the very people to whom Oliver Wendell Holmes referred when he lamented that they go to their graves with their music still inside.

We hope this book will awaken that sleeping giant by helping you—and people like you—to overcome the fears and uncertainty holding you back and allow you, through reflection and discernment, to find your passion, see your true potential, and act on it.

PART ONE:

LIVING MORE AND GIVING MORE

"We may not be able to do any great thing, but if each of us will do something, however small it may be, a good deal will be accomplished."

—D. L. MOODY, American evangelist and publisher, 1837–1899

Chapter One

THE BUTTERFLY EFFECT

I t was the flutter of a wing felt around the world. In 1963, Edward Lorenz presented his hypothesis about the "butterfly effect" to the New York Academy of Science. A butterfly could flap its wings on one side of the world and set molecules of air in motion which could then move other molecules of air. The cumulative effect had the potential to create a hurricane on the other side of the world.

The Academy laughed at the idea. But the concept, because it was so fascinating, endured. Physics professors in the mid-1990s established that it was accurate and valid. It proved true every time. And not just with butterflies and air molecules, but with all living matter, including people. Thus was established "the law of sensitive dependence upon initial conditions." In other words, a small impact on the initial conditions of a situation can greatly change the outcome.

Author and speaker Andy Andrews, in his book *The Butterfly Effect* and in his popular presentations, tells of hearing a television news program about Norman Borlaug, who was credited for saving the lives of over two billion people through his work producing corn and wheat hybrids for arid climates. Borlaug was awarded the Nobel Peace Prize in 1970 for significantly increasing the world's food supply.

Or was it Henry Wallace who really saved all those lives? Wallace was Franklin D. Roosevelt's second vice president; he previously had served as secretary of agriculture. As vice president, Wallace created a station in New Mexico that was dedicated to hybridizing corn and wheat for arid climates. To run it, he hired a young man named Norman Borlaug. So it was Henry Wallace who was the original source of this impactful discovery, then. He certainly seems to deserve at least some acknowledgment.

Unless, perhaps, it was George Washington Carver who saved those lives. You undoubtedly know about him for what he did with peanuts and sweet potatoes, developing them as alternative crops to provide nutrition and a spectrum of other products for poor Southern farmers. What you probably don't know is that when Carver was a student at Iowa State University, a dairy sciences professor let his six-year-old son accompany the brilliant student on weekend botanical expeditions. Carver befriended the boy and instilled in him a love of plants and a vision of what they could do for humanity. The boy's name was Henry Wallace.

George Washington Carver flapped his butterfly wings and touched the life of a boy who would grow into a man who helped change the world and save the lives of over two billion people. So it was Carver, then, who truly saved all those lives, right?

Unless, of course, it was a Civil War-era farmer from Diamond, Missouri, a man named Moses, and his wife, Susan. Susan had developed a close friendship with a slave named Mary Washington, who had an infant baby named George. One night, a group of night raiders kidnapped Mary and the baby. Susan was distraught over the loss of her friend and sent out word to learn what had become of her and the infant. Several days later, Moses was able to set up a meeting with the raiders at a crossroads to the north. He rode several hours on horseback and met four of the men, who showed up carrying torches and wearing burlap sacks over their heads with holes cut out for their eyes. He traded his horse for what they threw him in a dirty bag.

As the men thundered off on their horses, he got down on his knees, opened the bag, and took out a baby, cold and nearly dead. He put that frightened little child inside his coat next to his skin and wrapped him tightly, talking to him during the long walk home on that winter night. He and Susan vowed to raise him as their own and educate him. They gave that little boy their own family name, keeping his last name as his middle name in honor of his mother, who perished in the raid.

That is how Moses and Susan Carver came to raise baby George Washington Carver. And you can see how one easily could make the case that it was Moses and Susan Carver who saved those two billion souls.

This conversation could go on and on. And we could have such conversations about our own lives—our opportunities to influence those we touch now and for generations to come. It is important to remember that what we do matters, not just for ourselves and our families, but for our communities and—who knows?—perhaps even for all of humanity.

At the end of the classic Christmas movie *It's a Wonderful Life*, George Bailey's brother, Harry, toasts "the richest man in Bedford Falls" as friends and relatives stream into George's house to help him in his hour of need. George had been on the brink of suicide because of financial ruin until the angel Clarence gave him a rare opportunity to experience what his town and the lives of those he loved and cared for would be like had he never been born. George learned that night just how significantly he had touched, impacted, and transformed so many others during his own lifetime.

George Bailey, too—without even realizing it—had flapped his butterfly wings.

Are you being a good steward?

When we think of the concept of good stewardship, many of us tie it to our faith, whatever our belief system may be. We come to believe that our money and possessions aren't really ours. Rather it is all God's, or it is all part of the greater ethos of the universe, or whatever your beliefs might dictate. We are taught that our role is to be good stewards of what has been entrusted to us for the benefit of others. We are to consider those who will come after us, as we care for and use what we have been provided with.

Most individuals and families believe that stewardship begins with making sure they will grow and protect their wealth so it lasts for their lifetime and enables them to help their children and grandchildren. Some of us also understand a responsibility to be stewards for the needs of our community and the causes we believe in. But few people think deeply enough about this to make effective and strategic decisions about whether they're doing all that they can for what they really care about most. Many of us get so caught up in life's frenetic pace that our purpose unwittingly becomes "more" and "me"—mere accumulation, more material possessions, money for the sake of money.

We suddenly can find ourselves in a place of disillusionment, feeling confused or lost. Some call this a mid-life crisis; others identify it as depression. We may find ourselves missing the answers to these questions: "What is it really all about? What's my life purpose? What on earth am I here for?

How does this happen to us? We find ourselves rising early, managing the complexities of our lives on so many levels and ending too many of our days exhausted and, at times, overwhelmed. We seem to have little time just to stop, reflect, look up, look in, and listen.

Instead, we go through the motions—flip on the television, computer, phone, or tablet, for just a little while. As we do, we choose to ingest another constant parade of material offerings, allegedly newsworthy and relevant information—all topics supposedly important for "me and my life."

If we're really honest, most of this "consumption" leaves us with a vague undercurrent or emotion of fear and uncertainty—a general sense of angst and worry. And who could blame us? Especially after drops and uncertainty in the financial markets, political extremes reducing the effectiveness of the U.S. government, signs of global warming, the proliferation of terrorism, continued conflict around the world—and the beat goes on. As a result, most of us tend to pull back and draw inward. We revert to stockpiling mode, just in case. It sure seems as if the sky might be falling anytime now, doesn't it? We honestly don't feel safe. We're concerned there won't be enough.

In our practices this really is the case, even among our "wealthiest" clients. Some recall a childhood in the Depression, or have heard the stories of struggle, and they still fear that all they have could be gone tomorrow. Surveys have found that people with a net worth of $1 million to $10 million consider themselves middle class, not wealthy—they would need perhaps $50 million to feel that affluent. Those with $50 million would need $100 million to call themselves wealthy. And so on. You could say perceptions of wealth are a relative concept.

Here is the most important point to derive from this assessment: Most of us have lost a sense of clarity and confidence about our financial independence, what we really care about, and what we'd like to begin doing differently. Besides simply building more wealth and savings, how do we change our often-false perceptions about our wealth and financial freedom?

If you knew you could, wouldn't you?

It is a rhetorical question, because the answer is a given. If you knew you could, of course you would—it seems nobody would ever say otherwise. Any of us would if we honestly thought we could, right? The problem, however, is that all too many of us don't know this and don't believe we can.

From our professional experience, we have come to realize that the vast majority of us really do have proverbial diamonds in our own backyards. We really do have "excess wealth" that we don't know we have. If only someone would tell us, we would do something about it.

As a sage once said, we don't know what we don't know. But we can always choose to ask the tough questions and seek out truthful answers. We owe it to ourselves, our family, our legacy, and the future of whatever it is we care about most to discover whether we really can do more.

Right about now, you may be saying, "This sounds great and all, but how do I begin this kind of personal discovery process? How can I find my personal 'more that matters' and the financial capacity to make that happen? How do I begin creating my legacy of impact?"

The answer: with patience and persistence. Start out by putting one foot in front of the other. Follow the steps and guidance that we will provide in this book. Enlist the help of a skilled professional with the unique ability, experience, and process that you need to make progress.

Getting started on a new path, turning over a new leaf, or heading off in a new direction will almost always feel daunting at first. So be patient—with yourself and with the process. But if you are resolved and committed to finding honest answers, then begin. Pull out all the stops. Leave no rock unturned. Persist, persist, persist.

Many of our clients, like you, are wise about their resources and already have done some level of financial planning with one or more professionals. One common obstacle, however, is thinking that you are "all set." It is important to open yourself to the possibility that you don't really have it all figured out—that you haven't finished your plan. Because odds are, if you are like the majority of those we have had the privilege to serve over the years, you are not done yet.

For some of us, going into a professional's office feels like wading into a sea of complexity. We can feel intimidated, vulnerable, and even at risk of appearing stupid. "What if I haven't done something really basic, that I clearly should have managed by this point in my life?" We are concerned that we will be exposed for having missed the mark. The tax code is complicated. Financial, legal, and tax strategies can be even more confusing. Add investment products, estate plans, and words like *philanthropy*, and the experience threatens to overwhelm us.

But nobody knows it all. We all routinely delegate important and specialized segments of our lives and responsibilities to others who have more specific knowledge and expertise. Each of us has been blessed with our own strengths, personality attributes, areas of particular knowledge and heightened understanding, and unique skills and capabilities. If I needed heart surgery, would I perform it on myself? Of course not! If I wanted to build my dream house, would I draft the blueprint and build it myself? Not if I wanted to maximize my results.

Effective business leaders understand the concept of delegation. It is a key to successful leadership and achievement. The most accomplished and impactful people among us are highly skilled at strategically tapping into others' unique gifts and expertise. By employing the talents and skills of others, we thrive and our organizations thrive. This same principle holds true for each of us and our families.

Often the best way we can take our effectiveness to the next level is to hire competent, top-tier professionals who are specialists. We obviously are still the ones responsible. We're still the boss. We're still in control and make final decisions— but we're leaning upon far better, more reliable, and more strategic information. We're still conducting the orchestra— only with more well-tuned instruments available.

This is how you begin to discern your passions, your possibilities, and the specific opportunities that may be available to you. Whether it's retiring early to share and deepen your faith, volunteering for an organization you believe in, caring for your grandchildren, moving closer to your children or other loved ones, buying that lake house, traveling more and checking off experiences on that long bucket list, mentoring inner-city children at risk, serving somewhere meaningfully on the immense international stage, or . . .

If you hope to do more that matters to you personally, you need to tap into the insight, knowledge, and experience of those who can help you accomplish your goals clearly, confidently, efficiently, and effectively.

"If you haven't found something you are willing to die for, you aren't fit to live."

—MARTIN LUTHER KING, JR., civil rights leader, 1929–1968

Chapter Two

WHAT IS YOUR "MORE THAT MATTERS?"

Perhaps you have heard the story of Alfred Nobel, the Swedish chemist who invented dynamite. He was shocked to discover his own obituary published one morning in a French newspaper. He was very much alive—it was his brother, Ludwig, who had died, but the newspaper confused the two and, in doing so, described Alfred as a "merchant of death."

Nobel had thought his invention would end all wars. "The day when two army corps can annihilate each other in one second," he wrote, "all civilized nations, it is to be hoped, will recoil from war." Clearly, it appeared history would be judging him otherwise.

Unlike most of us, Nobel had been given the remarkable privilege of reading his own obituary—and he had a chance, from that day forward, to more intentionally and proactively write his own epitaph by creating the real legacy for which he hoped he would always be remembered. One of the first decisions he acted on was to better align his wealth with what he truly cared about most—human achievement. To do this, he changed his will, leaving everything he owned (when he actually did die) to establish the renowned Nobel prizes for accomplishments in a host of human endeavors.

Nobel obviously had been granted a very special second chance. If we're really honest, many of us would value such a wake-up call that provides a "do over" opportunity with our life and legacy. In Nobel's case, an erroneous obituary motivated him to focus intently on, bring to life, and actually *do* his personal "more that matters."

What will awaken and inspire the rest of us? Amidst the buzz and busyness of all of our lives, what will lead us to pause and reflect long enough on how we wish to be remembered? Thinking about how we'd like our epitaph to read and how we'd like to be remembered can be a helpful start. But perhaps even more importantly, we ought to reflect on what we personally feel led to touch, change, improve, impact, and provide with leadership during our lifetime. What will it take to get us to a place of decision and action?

Let's take our cue from Nobel's compelling story and begin living as if we're dying. *Carpe diem!* Seize the day! But not just for ourselves—for others. Why wait? As we all know, life is fragile and fleeting. Tomorrow may never come, and a meaningful, impactful life is the single best way to create a meaningful, impactful legacy. After all, the only legacy we can pass on after death is one that we have given life to while we are alive. Plus, it is a whole lot more fun to do our giving while we are living.

Your life as a "living legacy"

Darren Hardy, in his book *The Compound Effect*, discusses the power of your "why." If you were offered $20 to walk a 30-foot plank that was lying on the ground, he says, you would certainly accept such an easy challenge. But what if the plank were between the tops of two tall buildings? Would $20 be enough to take such a risk? Then imagine that you needed to cross that plank because the other building was burning and your children were in peril. Under such cir-cumstances, all of us would scramble across, without even a thought about money. This illustrates the power of deter-mining your "why"—understanding what motivates you to action.

Unless we find a source of motivation, energy, and inspiration—something truly important or even urgent—we won't take the action we ought to take. As humans, we are incredibly prone to procrastination or taking the path of least resistance. By and large, we avoid change and are slow to move toward new ideas and innovations. What we need is to see and understand our "why," opening ourselves up to different perspectives as well as new resources, searching and then focusing on how to move in the right direction.

Based on our combined 40 years of professional experience, we want to tell you, loud and clear: Yes, you can do this.

When we reflect back on the hundreds of individuals and families we have been fortunate to serve and advise, we can tell you with confidence that we're talking about saving and changing lives in ways that make your family, your community, and even the world a better place. And that's not hyperbole! Once you make up your mind that there is a compelling enough reason, you can rise to the challenge. So what is that reason for you?

If there's no good reason to cross that plank, you are unlikely to bother. If you (like so many others) see financial and estate planning as nothing more than a series of administrative or business decisions with lots of details needing to be managed, then you won't get to the place where Nobel was able to make his transformative decision. Your life will not become a living legacy if you only look at the risk of falling into the abyss; you will feel paralyzed and do nothing. But if you have a good reason, a really good reason, you will make it happen—and God knows there certainly is an abundance of really good reasons in this world. The personal way that you choose to respond to them is how you will write your epitaph and create your life and legacy.

Vision first, then goals

Vision must come first before specific goals can take shape. Admittedly, vision is a big, vague, and sometimes intimidating word. But it is also a very important amalgamation of our values, principles, ethics, and beliefs, as well as the outcomes we hope to make a reality. Preferably we can make this happen during life, but if not, then through our planning and our legacy.

"A man's worth is no greater than his ambitions."

–MARCUS AURELIUS, Roman philosopher and emperor, 121–180 CE

Chapter Three

THE THREE DIMENSIONS OF WEALTH

Take a moment to close your eyes and think about your five most important memories. What comes to mind?

We would guess your answers are about your family and life experiences. It is likely that none of them deal with money. You will recall, perhaps, your wedding day, or the birth of a child. It is not likely that you will find yourself musing about your dances with the Dow.

What do we really value most? We'd be wise to create an improved and more complete definition of wealth—because our wealth is about more than just money. What's your definition? Write it down. Then consider how you can work to enhance your wealth, as you have defined it. Because the goal is to amplify, expand, or "enhance" (as we like to call it) what you value most. Thus, the concept we most often focus on is planning to "enhance the wealth of your life and legacy."

When defining wealth, people usually think first in financial terms—the net worth statement, assets, liabilities, income, and expenses. The word "wealth" conjures up thoughts of money. And that, indeed, is one dimension of our wealth. But if you focus only on the financial dimension and ignore the personal and social dimensions, you likely will be missing the whole picture. And you also may miss discovering the "something" that motivates, energizes, and inspires you enough to take your planning to the next level.

You see, not all plans are created equal. Most, if we're honest, are one-dimensional in that they focus only on retirement planning or only on death and taxes. Most planning, frankly, isn't really planning at all. Instead it's some investments here, tax liabilities there, estate planning documents somewhere else, and then a whole bunch of hopes, fears, and dreams (usually never articulated to a professional) strewn about everywhere. A whole plan is not often illustrated and depicted in a comprehensive and integrated manner, incorporating "big picture" financial projections and analytics. As such, there is usually no real coordination or sense of understanding of how it all fits together.

We encourage you to create a three-dimensional plan— one that connects your financial, personal, and social dimensions of your wealth—allowing you to see, measure, monitor, and refine it. This is, by nature, detailed and involves many important elements that you must manage well to be smart and strategic. But how do we proactively make the best decisions, if it is almost impossible to see the forest for the trees?

The financial dimension

How will I grow and protect my wealth? Will I have enough savings to secure a long-term income through all my retirement years? Which investments and other financial solutions make the most sense for me? Who can I trust for financial advice? Do they have my best interest or a sale in mind? What tax strategies are safe, and which are too aggressive for my liking? These are the live-by-the-numbers decisions you make in the financial dimension of wealth planning.

However, by now, we hope you have started to accept the notion that the financial dimension is just one part of your wealth. It is obviously foundational and critical—you want to be certain you will have the money you need to support you and your family. But in many families the finances become the singular focus and can lead to something quite the opposite of financial freedom. It is more like an obsession, leading to insecurity, worry, and anxiety.

Unfortunately, though many of us have a real capacity to be using our good fortune to live more and to give more, we don't know it yet. We can't see the way things really are because we're stuck in our one-dimensional wealth boxes. The view is pretty poor from in there.

The truth is, millionaires abound in America, as Dr. Thomas J. Stanley observed in his seminal book *The Millionaire Next Door*. Most drive used cars. They're not dressed in Armani suits. They don't own the latest gadgets. They embrace a general value system of thriftiness; they don't carelessly throw things away, particularly money. They have a fix-it mentality. No wonder they have money: They don't spend like drunken sailors, and they are very good at saving. If they didn't experience the Depression, they took to heart the stories handed down to them. Some call these people the "blue-collar wealthy" or the "average affluent."

And this, too, is part of their value system: They tend to care about more than just themselves. They would rather give a dollar to their kids or to a cause than spend it on themselves. And they have a lot to give. Through being frugal in their spending and by making sure they're good stewards, they have accumulated substantial wealth, in relative terms. While they certainly would appear to have mastered the financial dimension of wealth, the values and good habits they've formed around their money can sometimes leave them keeping more than they need or ought to in their virtual mattress. They risk missing out on the life and legacy they desire because they can't look beyond the financial dimension of wealth, see things differently, and begin acting more freely on behalf of what they care about most.

One of our very early clients was a couple in their 70s who had considered hiring us to design and construct what we call a Life & Legacy Plan. However, they never wound up taking action. Some months later, the wife came in to see us. Her husband had died, and she hired us to administer his estate and then design a plan for her.

In a subsequent meeting to review the estate assets, we noticed that she had started crying as we were reviewing the report. We naturally asked if she was all right and whether we had said something to upset her. She explained that she had no idea whatsoever that they had more than $5 million dollars in property. She had been convinced by her husband, who had managed their finances, that they were barely scraping by. Things were always seemingly tight. She had cut coupons and sought out sales for so many years.

She sat there that day thinking about, and then sharing her regret about, what could have been. How many vacations did they never take? How many experiences did they miss out on? How much life could they have shared together, but now couldn't? How much of a blessing could they have been in helping their children and grandchildren at different times? They were both very involved in their church and community, so she also naturally felt disappointment about the lost opportunities to help the various causes and organizations they cared about so deeply.

The lesson of that day—one that we unfortunately have seen too many times since—helped us to realize how little freedom even successful people at all wealth levels allow themselves. The very ethics of frugality and thrift that serve these "wealthy" people so well during the accumulation years can block them from the bigger thinking and changed habits that are needed during the legacy years.

The secret to this freedom can be found in recognizing that there are two more important dimensions to our wealth.

The personal dimension

The personal dimension of wealth is found in our physical and emotional good health. It is an abundance of close family and cherished friends. It is a spiritual richness of faith and all that comes with it. Many of the things that enrich us and make our lives more vibrant and enjoyable don't involve money.

To uncover your core beliefs about this personal dimension of your wealth, consider how you would complete the following sentence: *"When I have more money, I will* _____*."* In talking with our clients over the years about this question, we find the answers typically fall into two categories: dreams and what we call "lifeprints."

Dreams are all of those things people vow to do one day, but usually never get to. They will do or take care of such-and-such when they have more money. But when we talk with clients, we find that they often already are financially capable of doing those things now. They just have not given themselves the permission to do so, or they have not done the planning necessary to give them the confidence and clarity to take action. They are missing perhaps a trusted advisor who is imploring them to "go after it," whatever "it" might be. They go through their lives with these dreams and aspirations of what they would like to accomplish, but they fail to take the necessary steps to make them a reality.

"Lifeprints" are the lasting imprints or impressions you would like to leave on the world. In other words, what evidence will you leave behind that signifies, like fingerprints or footprints, that you have been here? Boy Scouts and Girl Scouts are taught to leave their campsite better than they found it. That is a principle that many of us live by: We hope to leave this world a little better off—better for our children and for society as a whole—than it was when we arrived. It is human instinct to want to leave that lifeprint on the people, communities, causes, and institutions we care about.

We hear it all the time from clients: "I wish I could make a change, but…" or "I'd like to do something different, but…" or "We'd love to buy a vacation home for the family, but…".

Maybe you have said similar things yourself, or at least thought them. Usually the "but" reveals that the speaker feels the aspiration would be financially impossible or irresponsible.

It is a shame when dreams about doing work that is more satisfying, creating lifeprints, or enjoying life more in specific ways are stopped cold by uncertainty, unnecessary guilt, or even fear. When we hear peoples' voices trail off without fully describing their dreams and lifeprints in full detail and living color, we ask them a question: "Why not?"

Sometimes, subconsciously, people don't even allow themselves to begin to dream because of their foregone conclusions and assumptions about the way things are today. And you know what they say about assuming! We need to get help from professionals in this area to really understand our financial capacity relative to our own dreams and lifeprints. Shame on us if we assume anything, especially if it holds us back. We owe it to ourselves and to those we love to do our homework and, while still being responsible, get ourselves clear and confident about what is possible and what is not.

But even before we can do that, we need to let ourselves dream a little. When it comes to dreaming, we need more "thinking" with imagination and detail. Unfortunately, in our hectic pace of life, we leave little or no room for this kind of reflective thinking—no space to capture and expand our thoughts and give texture and life to our dreams.

If we don't make space for real understanding and true reflection, the first possible negative result is a "fire, ready, aim" approach to life and legacy, instead of the recommended "ready, aim, fire" technique. The second and even worse potential result is that we can find ourselves stuck. If so, we may have stopped "firing"—acting, doing, changing—altogether.

This is precisely where the right professional and the right design-build planning process can help individuals and families. Good life and legacy advisors play a variety of important roles: as tax, financial, and estate experts, of course; but also, more subtly, they are sometimes part coach, counselor, cheerleader, and even psychotherapist. With broad knowledge on a wide variety of related and relevant topics, skill in communicating and teaching complex concepts, and an ability to empathize and encourage, he or she can help you to identify and articulate your dreams and also to discover the confidence and freedom to "just do it."

In his book *Have a Little Faith*, Mitch Albom receives an unusual request: His 82-year-old childhood rabbi asks him to prepare and deliver his eulogy at his death. In preparation for the eulogy, Mitch frequently visits the rabbi to learn more about him and to discuss his thoughts on life and faith. During one conversation, the rabbi informs Mitch about the fact that everyone has a "second death." After our physical death, we all reach a point, typically after two generations, where we fade from the memories of our family members to become just a name on the family tree. This point is our unfortunate "second death." Can you remember the names of your great-grandparents? Do you know something about them, what they liked to do, or were passionate about? Are you taking steps and actions now with your grandchildren or great-grandchildren to ensure they know your name and what you are passionate about?

We must take the time not only to appreciate the richness in our lives but to work toward passing along those qualities as part of our legacy. Our stories, our memories, our spiritual beliefs, our loves and laughs, our challenges and victories— those are all part of how we will be remembered. They are assets of a different kind and are as worthy of passing on as anything in our investment portfolio. If we do pass them on, perhaps then our great-grandchildren not only will know our first name but they'll know our passions. We will have made our mark for posterity.

The social dimension

The final dimension of wealth is the social dimension. One way or another, part of your wealth will go toward the betterment of society. What is the difference between a philanthropist and a taxpayer? A philanthropist is defined as a "benevolent supporter of human beings and human welfare." A taxpayer, by contrast, is someone who gives up a significant portion of his family wealth to support the government's approach to providing for the general welfare of our country.

Both support the general welfare of human beings, but in very different ways. Being a taxpayer requires no planning or signing of documents. It is involuntary philanthropy and allows other individuals and government leaders to direct where your social wealth and capital will go. To be a philanthropist, however, is voluntary and requires planning. But it also empowers us and gives us the freedom to do more that matters to us personally for our family, our community, and the causes and organizations we care about.

The question is this: Do you want to contribute voluntarily and choose how to make an impact on society that is personal and important to you? Or do you want to contribute involuntarily (more than legally required) through the taxing authorities instead, allowing the federal or state government to make that choice for you? You could do nothing in the way of estate planning and let more of your money go to the government than necessary—and it certainly will be distributed. But if you are like most of the people we advise, you believe that is not good stewardship, as it speaks nothing of your priorities and passions. You can control the ultimate taxation of your wealth and the use of your wealth for social good. Whether you are a voluntary or involuntary philanthropist will be determined by your action or inaction.

It is the careful blending of these three dimensions of wealth—financial, personal, and social—that will motivate and guide us to succeed in creating a lasting legacy for our loved ones.

PART TWO:

THINKING DIFFERENTLY

"We cannot solve our problems with the same thinking we used when we created them."

—**ALBERT EINSTEIN,** German-born theoretical physicist, 1879–1955

Chapter Four

WHY SO MANY OF US FALL SHORT

In his book *Drive*, Daniel Pink summarizes three primary motivators of human behavior—and none of them is money. The first one is autonomy. We want to be able to have the freedom to do as we wish, the way we wish, and independence from needing anything from anybody.

The second motivator is mastery. Golfers know there's only one reason to play the game: to get better. Otherwise, you would have to admit, it is a pretty strange game of hitting and chasing a ball. We all are driven to get better and better—and that includes becoming better human beings. We want to care more about others than ourselves.

The third and most important motivator is purpose. People want their lives to have purpose. Each of us wants to find meaning in our life on this earth.

The desire to give and to make a difference is part of what makes us uniquely human, but people very often do so much less than they could. It is not because they want to do less. It is not because they don't care. As we have explained, the single biggest reason people don't do more is they honestly don't believe that they can.

Somebody or something has instilled fear in them. They have a sense of uncertainty and a lack of clarity. Perhaps the fear came from having endured tough times. Or perhaps a financial consultant led them to believe they would run out of money if they didn't play their cards just right. The message is that you need to save more, you need to invest more—and that may be the case—but often it is not.

We help people plan in a way that leaves them crystal clear as to what they can do. When they attain that confidence, they start getting in the game with a sense of purpose. Can you really manage your finances and plan your estate in a meaningful, thoughtful way if you think you are going to run out of money? You are left thinking: "What am I planning for? There might not even be anything left. Why should I put in all this time and effort to get into a complex conversation where I have to share all of my private information, humiliate myself by sharing my past mistakes, and then even have to talk about my own death? Who knows if anything of substance is even going to be left?"

When you have clarity and confidence that something indeed will be left—in many cases, something substantial— then you feel more motivated to plan. You begin to think about the possibilities you may have for more impactful living and giving.

When we speak about philanthropy in public venues, people nod their heads all across the room when asked whether they would like to do more for something they care about. Why aren't they doing so? "I've been meaning to get around to it." Or, "I'm not really sure about the best way to go about doing this." Sometimes, they don't really know. "I guess I'm nervous," they may say, or "I'm worried." It all points to that lack of confidence.

"What's philanpoppy?"

The "millionaires next door" often do not relate, at first, to the possibilities of philanthropy—until they see that they can do it voluntarily so the government doesn't make them do it involuntarily. That realization appeals to those innate human drives for autonomy, mastery and purpose.

"What's philanpoppy?" one client asked. He quickly learned—not only how to pronounce the word but also its many benefits. And today, he is quite active in his giving to his church, as well as several community charitable organizations he cares about. He also restated his trust, zeroing out federal estate taxes in favor of his family's chosen causes and organizations. Truth is, once the average affluent come to understand how philanthropy can work for them and their families, and that it is not just for the realm of the ultra-wealthy, they want to do more.

Understanding the efficiency—the fundamental frugality—of tax planning to promote philanthropy is quite reassuring to those millionaires next door, for whom frugality and efficiency are a way of life. When they come to see this is a legitimate means to give more to good causes without reducing what goes to their children, they are eager to pursue this strategy.

Still, most people have yet to discover that they can redirect what would have been paid in taxes to charity without reducing what is left to their family or heirs. This type of planning constitutes a large untapped source of potential funding for nonprofit organizations. The millionaires next door tend to show, along with the other values that brought them their wealth, a staunch independence. They are not big fans of the idea of allowing the government to collect more in taxes than it needs, all because the government's poor planning resulted in their paying more taxes then were required. When they see that philanthropy lets them redirect those taxes as they see fit (within certain parameters, of course), they feel empowered. The idea matches their mindset. They can do their own thing. It even feels entrepreneurial. Soon they want to do more than just redirect taxes—they very often begin to develop a passion for the causes they are helping.

"But I'm not Bill Gates"

Many people whom society would regard as well-off are actually concerned about running out of money. And that fear is part of the challenge in encouraging them to engage in philanthropy. The media hardly helps the situation: Advertisers, in their bid for attention, take things to the extreme and play on those worries. You can see this daily as the financial news networks proclaim that the financial markets are in a boom or that there is gloom and doom ahead. Affluent people come to feel insecure—they could lose all their money or there could be a global economic collapse. The sky always seems to be falling. Feeling so vulnerable, how could they risk helping others? In truth, if you consider yourself able to help the world, then you are able to help the world. Generosity is an attitude, a way of life.

You don't have to be Bill Gates. The Microsoft founder has so much excess wealth that he built one of the largest grant-making nonprofit organizations in the world. We're not suggesting that you go out and create a huge grant-making nonprofit. We're just saying you may be able to do a little something more, or a lot more, than you are doing currently. What is it you want to do? What do you care about? What have you long dreamed about?

Do more that matters. You can do it through giving, through living, or through both—and it certainly doesn't need to be on a Bill Gates scale.

It doesn't have to even be about money. It is rewarding to see clients gain the clarity and confidence to know that they can retire so that they can spend more time doing the volunteer work they love to do, redirecting their marketplace acumen and experience toward charitable and nonprofit organizations and causes. For example, one retired couple we know travel around the country in an RV working for Habitat for Humanity. They go south in the winter and north in the summer, using their skills and labor to help break the cycle of poverty, one house at a time.

Even if you can't write a check with multiple zeros on it, you can still make a significant impact. Don't forget what the flutter of one butterfly's wings can bring forth.

How much do I really need?

Many people could easily write big checks, but something holds them back. Most of our clients are age 60 and over and have a net worth generally in the range of $1 million to $30 million dollars. They could spend hundreds of thousands of dollars more than they spend now, but they can't bring themselves to do it. When shown that they have excess wealth, they might travel more or perhaps buy a second home, but they're not likely to do a whole lot more than that. It is just not who they are.

Ask yourself this: How much do I really need for what I'm going to do? Is my goal to see how much money I can pile up? Or do I want to leave my mark on how it is spent, on what my money can do?

Here's the truth about legacy planning and philanthropy: Including a charity or nonprofit in your planning does not have to mean that you will leave less to your family. One does not need to exclude the other. It can be done through alternative methods that are quite legitimate. It is just not the traditional way that most people plan.

By taking advantage of incentives that are in place—and that aren't typically employed in traditional planning—you can leverage your money for what you care about. Most people don't know about these strategies. For example, most people don't know that at the federal level you can zero out your estate taxes. How? By diverting what would have gone to the government to your chosen causes and organizations. It is a zero-sum game: What the federal government loses in taxes, nonprofits gain in legacy-creating contributions.

Let's emphasize again: Your philanthropy can be voluntary, or it can be involuntary. The government is a kind of quasi-charity. It is a social organization. Through taxes, your money is going into the social capital funnel. In our experience, most families don't want their hard-earned savings to go there. It is not because they're unpatriotic— they just don't think government programs and spending is the most efficient way to get their money to where they believe it is needed the most. They want to maintain control of the impact they have with their wealth.

Why, then, don't people do more, if these methods are legitimate and well within their grasp? Often it is as simple as this: Most people are under the misconception that every dollar left to charity is a dollar less that their family will receive. They see all their goods and assets as if they were part of a pie, and if somebody else gets a slice of that pie, the other portions will be smaller.

It doesn't work that way. Through a variety of strategies—financial, legal, tax, and leveraging techniques—we can make the pie and its slices bigger. That is the virtue of the comprehensive strategy we call Life & Legacy Planning. Just one slice of the bigger pie can actually feed more people than the entire smaller pie.

Your children or beneficiaries don't have to end up with less. Quite frankly, through proper planning, they often can end up with more, if that is what you want. When people come to understand that providing for charitable causes does not require them to shortchange their heirs at all, they feel a new freedom to reach out with a helping hand.

Procrastination

It is one thing to feel that freedom, however, and another to take action. Though convinced they should take their plan to the next level, create a legacy, and make an impact by possibly engaging in philanthropy, people procrastinate for a host of reasons. And they aren't necessarily conscious that they are doing so.

The biggest reason to procrastinate is our sense of mortality. As noble as a cause may be, the thought of leaving your money leads to the thought of dying. It can seem like planning for one's own demise—not the most comfortable of feelings. Rather than face that truth, people tend to find a whole lot of other things they can do.

And frankly, people procrastinate out of a fear they will discover that their pile of money just isn't big enough after all. They lack a clear understanding of their own finances or don't access the professional guidance that would help them gain it. Will there be enough money to live on for the rest of their lives? Will there be anything left for the kids? Will they have the resources to face an emergency or an illness? They just don't know. As a result, they're reluctant to take a closer look. So they put their heads in the sand in a misbegotten effort to avoid the threats that very well might not be there at all.

Insecurity also plays a role. Revealing your finances can feel like being stripped of your clothes. Will everyone see the woeful state of your planning? It is the reason that many people avoid their annual physicals. Everything's out there in the open, and what if the doctor has some stern words for you? Often, the doctor has reassuring words—and such may well be the case for those who seek out advice on whether they can engage in life and legacy planning and philanthropy.

In some families, such planning raises the specter of unresolved family issues. It can be painful, in such cases, to broach the subject of whether to leave money to the children or how much. How is it to be done fairly? There may be concerns about the stability of relationships and marriages and the status of stepchildren.

Many families today are dysfunctional, unable to work through their problems and communicate well—and so there's a tendency to let sleeping dogs lie. But if there is a compelling reason to steer money away from a particular individual in the family, good planning is crucial. He or she may benefit from your procrastination. How much better would it be to leave money to a worthy person or cause?

Sometimes though, people just get caught up in their day-to-day living. They appreciate the concept of creating a legacy and making an impact, but it plays no immediate role in getting through a day. Legacy and philanthropy can, for some, seem to be all about the future and about others—it doesn't seem to affect how well they are faring in the here and now. It's just more details to manage, and there's no sense of urgency. That is a limited perspective, of course. Proper planning in this arena most certainly can enhance your lifestyle—not to mention the lifestyles of many others. But it might not seem that way, and so it is easy to put off.

What awakens the need to take action? It could be the death of a loved one, leading you to reflect on what that person would have wanted—and what you really want. It could be a job loss, or an illness. At some point, whatever it is, your impact and your legacy become more of an imperative than just a load of administrative details. Something in life becomes the game changer that makes you think deeply about what matters most to you and to those around you.

The lack of a financial plan

Many people spend more time and care planning their vacations than they spend on their financial and estate planning. They will pore over travel guides and find the best rates online, all in anticipation of a week or two in their future. Probably because of our human impulses, planning for short-term fun can trump long-term gain. With the future uncertain, risks to be managed, a retirement for which we fear we may not have saved enough, and worse yet, death and taxes, many of us understandably lack the requisite enthusiasm and courage to address this area of planning with commitment, energy, and urgency.

If you don't know where you are going, any road will get you there. To plot a course for a significant legacy, you first need a plan for yourself. Only then will you have the confidence and clarity to plan for others.

One of people's biggest fears, particularly as they approach retirement age, is that they won't have enough money for themselves. They may wonder whether they might end up as somebody else's charity case. That fear may be justified or it may be unfounded—and comprehensive financial planning will resolve any doubts. For some reason, people are prone to making presumptions about these things that simply aren't based on facts or sound analysis.

Emotion and gut instinct are hardly a reliable guide when it comes to your financial freedom (or lack thereof). We cannot accurately see where we are heading or what greater things might be possible if we don't know where we are at this moment. It is not unlike using a GPS, that navigation tool we all are familiar with in some format. The technology is dependent on two critical inputs: current location and chosen destination.

Investment and asset management has been around for a long time, but financial planning as a professional discipline has been around for only about 30 years. And not everyone who calls this service financial planning is doing the same thing. There is a wide spectrum of approaches and of quality. As a result, very few people have a well-constructed and complete plan.

With a current approach to planning, you actually may find you already can do far more than you think. One client of ours, the founder and principal of an executive coaching firm, had a net worth of approximately $10 million. He owned valuable property in Boston and on a lake in New Hampshire, with no mortgage on either. He had a solid income and sizable investment portfolio. Finally, he was a board member of a Fortune 100 company and expected to be paid a seven-figure executive compensation benefit at the end of his term as a director.

He and his wife were motivated and intrigued with the idea of being more intentional and artful with their family legacy—and also by the prospect of becoming more active and impactful philanthropically. We estimated for him that he could leave a philanthropic legacy of seven figures plus. His existing investment advisory firm, however, had left them with the idea that they would be lucky if their children inherited a few hundred thousand dollars—and that they faced a real risk of not having enough assets to provide themselves with long-term retirement income for the remainder of their lifetimes.

It turned out that his well-respected investment advisory firm had produced an "ultra-conservative" retirement analysis that was designed to build confidence, even in a doomsday scenario, about their financial independence. Unfortunately, the firm did not create a comprehensive plan to help the family see the more likely scenario from an estate and legacy planning perspective.

Sometimes, a "conservative" retirement-only analysis can be the equivalent of a quite "aggressive" estate analysis, in terms of tax exposure and other risks. The firm left the couple feeling fearful about their retirement, and, as such, they hadn't even begun to consider family legacy or philanthropy in any meaningful way.

How did this happen? The firm had disregarded the value of the couple's two properties, the value of his coaching business, and the value of the executive compensation plan. Of his $10 million net worth, $7 million (which was not liquid at the time of the retirement analysis) had been ignored in the illustration that the firm created. Unfortunately, such an experience is not uncommon. Such incomplete planning holds back many people from doing more.

And, as you can see from this real-life example, the marketplace doesn't always provide a planning product or service that helps us to get to this important place of doing more. Working with the right advisor can make a tremendous difference, creating a greater impact and allowing you to live more and give more.

*"Our chief want is someone who will inspire
us to be what we know we could be."*

—RALPH WALDO EMERSON, American essayist and poet, 1803–1882

Chapter Five

HOW FINANCIAL PROFESSIONALS CAN GET IN THE WAY

"We have met the enemy, and he is us." So observed Pogo, the philosophical possum and title character in Walt Kelly's long-running comic strip of social and political satire set in the Okefenokee Swamp.

In the world of financial professionals, a major obstacle to getting people to do more is, unfortunately, the professionals themselves. Frequently, professionals such as attorneys, investment advisors, insurance professionals, and accountants tell us their clients aren't interested in charitable giving but instead want to minimize taxes and maximize the wealth that their family and heirs will receive.

How does the financial professional industry in general come to this conclusion that people don't want to support personal causes and organizations? The most common basis for this assertion is: "I asked them, and that's what they told me." When questioned about how they asked, we usually hear some variation of this not-so-creative or sophisticated question: "Do you want to leave money to charity?" And the response they usually elicit is about what you'd expect.

Such a blunt question seems to dredge up those primal concerns in people about whether there's enough for them and whether there's likely to be anything left for the family. Even if those are not direct concerns, there is rarely any explanation or education to clarify the common misconception most people have: that a charitable legacy means the family will receive less than it would otherwise.

The vast majority of professional advisors have little to no experience in how to facilitate an engaging and productive conversation on legacy planning and philanthropy. Here are some fairly simple and effective questions that advisors could ask their clients to develop this important conversation:

- "If you knew you could afford to give more to causes and organizations you personally care about, without compromising your financial independence and lifestyle, would this be interesting and potentially valuable to you?"

- "Were you aware that in most circumstances, when you leave money to charity through your estate or trust, it does not have to reduce your family's share?"
- "Would you prefer to take the portion of your money that otherwise would be paid to the government in taxes after your death, and instead redirect those assets to your personally chosen causes and organizations?"

These three questions are much more likely to help people begin thinking differently and dispelling whatever ignorance or misconceptions they may have toward this subject. Ultimately, with just a bit more thought and care, professionals can guide and counsel clients in ways that encourage and empower them to get into a game they do in fact care about, but never really thought they could afford to play.

Instead, most advisors unwittingly (or in some cases, not so unwittingly) tap into or add to people's already existing fears. They don't explain the difference between voluntary and involuntary philanthropy. When people regularly respond, "Well, no, we'll need that money for us and the kids," many financial professionals conclude that the conversation is over. Additionally, they feel this is a conversation that just isn't worth having unless the client brings it up.

At the risk of introducing another profession to make an important analogy, we'd ask you to consider whether the best advisors should act as pharmacists or as physicians? Should your advisor just *dispense* the prescriptions or solutions to the issues you bring to him or her? Are you expected to depend on the answers you receive, without question? Or do you want your advisor to be ready, willing, and able to have the kind of courageous conversations that a good physician should be free to initiate?

Haven't the most helpful people in our own lives been the advisors, mentors, counselors, and friends who have asked us the best and sometimes most compelling questions? Do we routinely label someone "wise" who has that admirable trait of habitually asking that one extra question that others don't ask? Don't we respect most those who help us challenge our own assumptions and sometimes our stubbornness?

Aren't advisors smarter and infinitely more helpful to their clients if they clearly discuss the scope of the proverbial "medications and treatments" (i.e. strategies, solutions, investments, etc.) that can truly improve the quality of their life and legacy—as a skilled and compassionate physician would?

In truth, many of the individuals and families we serve, who trust us and rely on us, just don't really appreciate or know on their own what they can accomplish through their legacy and philanthropic planning. Wouldn't the best advisors want their clients to know this? And if one of your advisors helped you realize this, wouldn't you trust and rely on them that much more in the future?

Advisors of many stripes

You will hear many labels for those who want to counsel you on how to use and invest your money: financial advisors, financial consultants, financial planners, investment managers, investment advisors. By any name, they all purport to do planning. You can discern much about the nature of that planning by considering how the advisor is compensated. That also can have a significant influence on the type of advice you get.

Some advisors are compensated exclusively by up-front commissions—and that is like hiring someone to renovate your kitchen and paying the whole project cost up front before seeing the quality of the work. With a commission, the advisor is in effect being paid up front for services to be done in the future. And since the compensation comes in advance, the advisor has less of an incentive to do the ongoing, important work of recommending adjustments and refinements, or changes to your plan, investments, or other strategies in the future.

Life happens, laws change, and family dynamics are unpredictable. We could go on and on about the impor-tance of maintaining a viable plan or the specific tactics a client may have put in place. Advisors compensated strictly by up-front commissions face a significant hurdle in being able to deliver service. In addition, the advisor continually must bring in new investments in order to maintain his or her income. As a result, less attention gets paid to monitoring your plan because, quite frankly, it becomes something that is difficult to afford.

In many ways, the asset management fee model—in which financial advisors get paid an annual percentage of the value of the assets they manage and retain each year—is a good one. After all, the investor wants to make money and the advisor is all in favor of that because he or she gets paid for the value they provide. The incentives of the advisor and the client seem most often to be aligned; this translates into growing the account value. It is an arrangement that has worked well for the vast majority of financial advisors for a long time.

If financial planning is offered, asset managers often don't charge a separate fee for that planning. They include it in their asset management fee. And these days, with ever-shrinking margins being demanded of the investment advisory marketplace, while volatile financial markets cause some clients to need more attention, service and hand-holding than ever before, anything extra that is being added to the overall service offering has become that much more difficult to afford and sustain. The "no free lunch" adage applies here: You usually don't get the same level of planning when it is being added to the compensation for "no additional cost" or worse yet, for free.

So the quality and sophistication of what is called "planning" in the marketplace varies greatly from one advisor and financial firm to another. Too often, the plans being produced are nothing more than investment analysis or retirement plans. Additionally, many of these professionals are designing plans that, quite frankly, serve to keep the assets under management long term.

Ultra-conservative is usually a good approach to projecting investment returns and retirement income, but one must question when the line is crossed from being conservative to being a bit self-serving. You see, it is in the interest of advisors following this old model to both gather and retain assets under management. It is not in their best interest to recommend that you live more or give more of your assets away. If and when they do, they also are encouraging you to live or give away a portion of their future income.

It is our firm belief that the most valuable thing an advisor can design and refine from year to year is a holistic, multidimensional, comprehensive Life & Legacy Plan. This is the blueprint. This is the schematic report. This is the operating system, or instruction manual. This is the only way to effectively see and continue to see the whole landscape. Isn't this what is most valuable of all?

The planning fee is best kept separate. It should be a good value on its own merits, regardless of the investment management. This is the only reliable way to foster and maintain true objectivity. The client's goals should drive the decisions. The plan must prove that a particular recommendation makes strategic sense in light of the client's objectives. This avoids the risk that the hidden driver or motivation for a proposed action is instead the advisor's desires related to his or her compensation.

Failure to see the big picture

A high percentage of financial advisors come from the worlds of investment management or life insurance. Unfortunately, they often do not have the breadth of knowledge about planning that you may need. They tend to gravitate toward their own world, one way or another. They may have deep expertise, but if so, this often is tied to their area of specialty and does not usually extend more broadly across the various areas that need to be addressed in a typical plan design. One recommends insurance products regularly, and the other suggests an array of investment strategies and recommendations. Neither is usually equipped to offer the big picture.

Sometimes they also can become inclined, after years of practice, to do things the same way for all their clients. Square pegs shouldn't be forced into round holes. You are not getting a customized plan. Such advisors may lean on a particular investment firm or insurance company as an information source and/or product sponsor. They use the tools at hand—and to a hammer, everything looks like a nail.

When it comes to legacy and charitable planning, it is even more important to work with a specialist who understands the kind of detailed planning required for growing and protecting an estate and carefully passing it on.

As in the medical profession, specialists focus on your differing needs. Likewise, there are many good attorneys who supposedly do estate planning, but in reality they often focus on a wide variety of aspects of the law. The day of the general practice attorney has long passed. Buyers most certainly should beware if and when you are working with this type of attorney for assistance with your estate. There simply is too much information to know and remain current with; there are too many minefields to cross, and too many mistakes that can be made.

Even when working with an attorney who specializes in estate planning, the plain reality is that they are not trained for, nor do they typically have, a business model that supports running projections, crunching numbers, producing the graphs and reports that help bring the requisite clarity and confidence you need to make big decisions and put in place meaningful and impactful provisions. For estate, legacy, and philanthropic planning, you need a specialist who can help you view the entire picture; determine your heartfelt intentions, goals, and passions; and help you overcome whatever challenges may get in the way.

That being said, an advanced estate planning attorney who is familiar with legacy and philanthropic planning is an indispensable member of the professional planning team. The finer elements of drafting legal provisions, navigating jurisdictional nuances in the law, and interpreting applicable tax court cases and regulations often are critical in implementing a plan that will work as designed.

Insurance pros vs. investment pros

Life insurance professionals often will tell you that they do a lot of estate planning. To them, that means you should buy life insurance because your estate will be subject to estate tax—and the death benefit will provide liquid money to pay that tax. That way, your estate will remain intact for the benefit of your loved ones, not the government. Life insurance lets you protect what could be a substantial estate in exchange for a relatively low premium. And that seems to make sense. Certainly paying pennies in taxes is preferable to dollars. The concept of leveraging insurance premium payments to provide a larger death benefit for estate protection in this manner has been around for many years and is widely accepted as a common strategy used by taxable estate holders.

However, most people who say "yes" to such a strategy don't realize that there is an even more compelling alternative—creating a zero estate-tax plan. While the "insurance to pay taxes" plan makes some sense, it still involves sending substantial dollars to the taxing authorities unnecessarily. If you can eliminate those taxes altogether by including a charitable legacy, then life insurance can become potentially even more exciting as a method to significantly support the people, causes, and organizations you care about most. The strategy then becomes one of pursuing the good instead of avoiding the bad.

Nevertheless, most life insurance professionals don't talk to you about zero estate-tax planning. To them, the estate tax is a good thing because it creates a need for the liquidity that you can gain from what they are selling.

Meanwhile, if you talk to investment professionals, you very often will find them antagonistic toward life insurance products, including annuities. One reason may be that they don't have a life insurance license, which is required for them to work with these types of financial products. That means they can't make money on insurance products, so why would they recommend them?

Also, because there would be less money invested with them, they would receive less in annual asset management fees. Today, some of the large investment firms have started to deal with insurance strategies, as if to say, "If you can't beat them, join them." At the same time, they lack the sophistication, knowledge, and professionalism in this area that they may demonstrate on the investment side. The hallmark of a good professional will be an advisor that can provide both investment and insurance services, or has relationships to collaborate with other advisors.

With the marketplace seemingly divided between investment and insurance strategies, you wind up caught in the middle, trying to find confidence and a more balanced and accurate understanding of what you have to sort out from all these many opinions that you hear. We believe the advisor's ultimate goal must be helping you and those like you to live more and do more for what you care about. Whatever products, strategies or solutions make the most sense in this pursuit and best support this overarching goal is what you should be implementing.

To do this, professionals who are working within one of these old traditional models should consider becoming life and legacy planners or collaborating with one. Why? Because this is the only honest and real way to improve the competence and ability needed to take your planning to the next level and to act with integrity about what truly is in your best interest.

Don't succumb to fear

The financial industry gains by engendering fear. Will you have enough to retire? Can you provide for your family? The industry tends to play on people's insecurities and their desire to gain as much as possible in hopes of driving away those anxieties. The industry gets paid to manage money, and the bigger that pile of money, the bigger the management fee. It can become all about the pursuit of more, rather than about more that matters.

Too many financial advisors are product-centered salespeople. If they are good at this type of sales, they use a sense of urgency about what they want to sell to compel you to buy their products, rather than help you to pursue what might be the most strategic approach. Many of those salespeople are taught and trained to feed the fire of fear—because fear sells. Decisions often are driven by emotion, and salespeople of this type recognize that fear is a mighty motivator.

But we can get beyond those fears. Once we do, we may be able to discover a compelling truth: We have the means to amply provide for our own financial needs and more. What will that more be for? By replacing fear with freedom, through the clarity and confidence that emerges from a precisely designed and complete plan and supporting analysis, we are empowered as the ones who now can decide. No longer should we accept being captive to the lead of a one-dimensional advisor or an industry with competing objectives. We can *be* more and *do* more.

What to look for in an advisor

Here are some suggestions about how to find an advisor to assist you with planning and beginning to do your more that matters.

In creating a list of possible advisors, you may begin by asking friends for referrals, reviewing articles or books you have read, or conducting searches on the Internet. As we mentioned earlier, it is important to look for a specialist in legacy, life, charitable, or philanthropic planning. A common place to start may be to look for an advisor with a professional designation, such as a Certified Financial Planner Professional (www.cfp.net), or by searching for individuals associated with organizations such as the Financial Planners Association (www.fpanet.org) or the National Association of Personal Financial Advisors (www.napfa.org).

Well-trained and highly regarded consortiums of estate planning attorneys also exist nationally. Finding an attorney who is a member of one of those groups can help you with your due diligence as you decide who to work with. These include: WealthCounsel (www.wealthcounsel.com), the American College of Trust and Estate Counsel (www.actec. org), The National Network of Estate Planning Attorneys (www.nnepa.com) as well as the American Academy of Estate Planning Attorneys (www.aaepa.com).

Once you have identified a professional with whom you may want to work, first spend some time meeting the advisor to determine his or her focus. During your first meeting, assess whether the advisor is doing all of the talking, or if he or she is helping you think about your situation, maybe even your goals, dreams, and concerns. If the advisor does the majority of the speaking or only talks about what he or she does, then the focus is not on you. Also, note whether the advisor is guiding you to the charitable possibilities you may have. Does the advisor take the time to explore your interest in doing more that matters? The first job of a life and legacy planning specialist is to help you determine what is really important to you and what you care about most.

Second, do you understand the advisor? Is he or she speaking with you in a language you understand, or just using terminology and industry jargon, perhaps in an attempt to impress you? The best planners will be able to explain the process in a simple-to-understand manner. It also is important to find out how extensive the advisor's planning capability is in the areas of financial, tax, and estate planning. Will you be able to get assistance with the three dimensions of your wealth, to focus on your dreams and lifeprints, or will the focus strictly be on your financial dimension, just sticking to the numbers?

Lastly, discuss how the advisor is compensated. As we discussed previously, a good financial advisor will be compensated for the planning that he or she designs and maintains for you. The compensation should not be tied to investment management fees or other product commissions such as life insurance alone. The plan is the most valuable part, so the best advisors will acknowledge this by charging a separate fee for this service. It should not be a nominal fee, but a fairly significant fee. This demonstrates a commitment to objectivity and an alignment with the idea that the plan is what is most important.

Savvy individuals and families should require prospective advisors to estimate the anticipated value they can expect in exchange for any proposed planning fee. None of us has any particular aversion to spending money. We all do it every day. What we do care about, however, is getting a good value. This area is no different. In some ways, it is even more acute. We should be more than happy to "invest" in a planning fee like this when the substantial anticipated value (not just more money, but a variety of desired outcomes that you care about most) is the byproduct.

If you are currently working with an advisor who either does not provide or is not proficient in philanthropic planning, consider engaging an additional advisor specializing in this area or meeting with another advisor for a second opinion or review of your current financial plan.

Finding a great planner to assist you in determining your passion, your goals, and your dreams—and then designing and refining a plan that enables you to see and create the very real possibilities you desire for your future—may take some time. But it is worth it, because the results can be amazing—even life-changing.

"The saddest words in the
English language are 'if only.'"

—**ZIG ZIGLAR,** American author and motivational speaker, 1926-2012

Chapter Six

PLAN WITH A BIGGER END IN MIND

O ctober 5, 1941: It's the final out of Game 4 of the World Series, and the Brooklyn Dodgers hold a 4–3 lead over the Yankees at Ebbets Field. Brooklyn is poised to tie the series at two games each. At the plate is Tom Henrich, a star Yankee outfielder, with no men on base. At the mound is ace reliever Hugh Casey. Casey's pitch breaks sharply, and Henrich swings and misses. The umpire calls the out, and the game seems over.

But the ball skips off the heel of catcher Mickey Owen's glove, and as he chases it, Henrich races to first. Up next is Joe DiMaggio, who singles. Charlie Keller then bats them in to give the Yankees a 5-4 lead. Then they score two more, and the Dodgers go down quickly in the ninth. Heading into Game 5 with a lead of three games to one, the Yankees win the title the next day.

Mickey Owen's error cost the Dodgers the game and, as many would see it, the series. Would anyone remember or particularly care that until then he'd had a superb season, with no errors?

And years later, who would talk about his amazing career? If it was mentioned, it was almost in passing. Mostly, people talked about what he had done to the Dodgers. "I would have been completely forgotten," he said years later in an interview, "if I hadn't missed that pitch."

Owen died July 13, 2005, and here's how the *New York Times* began his obituary:

> ### *Mickey Owen Dies at 89;*
> ### *Allowed Fateful Passed Ball*
> *Mickey Owen, the Brooklyn Dodger catcher remembered for a misadventure in the 1941 World Series that propelled the Yankees to the championship and overshadowed his All-Star career, died Wednesday at a nursing home in Mount Vernon, Mo. He was 89. The cause was complications of Alzheimer's disease, his son, Charles, said.*
>
> *Owen played for 13 seasons in the major leagues and was an outstanding catcher with a strong, accurate arm. But he has been linked in baseball history with figures like Fred Merkle, Ralph Branca and Bill*

Buckner, all outstanding players defined by a single moment of misfortune.

When it comes to reflecting on our personal situations, lives, and future legacies, none of us wants a "Mickey Owen" to happen to us. Many of us have spent decades working hard, trying to save and build our net worth. We certainly don't want to be remembered by the one thing we didn't do right. We need to make sure the generations ahead know who we truly were. We must not someday leave our family feeling that we dropped the ball by not managing our financial and estate planning more carefully and thoughtfully.

Nothing is certain but death and taxes, according to an old aphorism. In most areas of financial planning, there are certainly a good many variables. When it comes to estate planning, you can say for certain that at some point in the future each of us will surely die. Nonetheless, most Americans do not take the appropriate steps to plan for this inevitability. If we only knew when that fateful day would befall us, we could manage these important details just in time. Putting it off as long as possible is what many of us seem to do. For example, a 2007 survey, performed by Harris Interactive of Martindale-Hubbell, found that 6 out of 10 Americans do not have even a will in place.

In many families, relationships are torn apart by disagreements and battles over financial assets after someone passes away. Your failure to adequately plan could turn out to be more than just a bad reflection on you—it could truly hurt your family as a consequence, destroying previously strong and healthy relationships. And, of course, it need not be that way. There is really no excuse for any of us. There is plenty that can be done simply by having a game plan.

Preparing an estate plan

In preparing that game plan as it pertains to your estate, the first step is to take the time to think through what you would like the end result to be. As with so many things in life, whether career or relationships, or even sports, you cannot achieve success unless you are clear about the desired end result. Defining success in your own terms is the only effective means to do this.

This same principle applies to your estate planning. It is important to think about the end first. If you were to pass away and your family members and friends were talking about you, what would you want them to say? What would you want your eulogy to express about the value you brought to this world and the impact that you had on others? What did you do that mattered?

We can break down the early steps of preparing an estate plan into soft points and hard points. A soft point is the discovery of what we truly want to achieve. Just as Alfred Nobel took bold steps so that he would be remembered as a voice for peace through human achievement and not a purveyor of war, we all should think carefully about our aspirations and what we feel is most important. Most people want to get down to brass tacks. They want to reach one plus one equals two as quickly and efficiently as possible.

They simply want to know, "What do I need to do?" There's obviously no solution that fits everyone. But by defining your ideal outcome and what success means to you, your goals and priorities begin to emerge, helping you assess where you stand now. You then can address the question of how to get from "here" to "there" as you begin to travel along that route more intentionally and with greater focus.

After those "soft" considerations, you will then be in a much better place to consider what we call the "hard" decisions—such as what to leave to whom, how to provide for your beneficiaries, and which legal documents and provisions are needed. During this process, attention must be paid to special circumstances and unique risks that may exist within your family or may be related to certain specific assets.

The primary purpose of creating your estate plan is to maintain control, whether it is putting legal documents in place to execute your wishes when you are unable to, or eventually after your death. It is important to consider the five core estate planning documents that are needed to maintain control of your decision making and ensure that your intentions will be honored during your life and beyond.

The initial step is to establish a will. This document will dictate who will inherit your assets and, if your children are underage, who will become their guardians. All wills are subject to a probate process in which the probate court follows a legal proceeding to take an inventory of your estate, make appraisals of any property, settle outstanding debts, and distribute the remaining assets. Without a will, you allow state law to dictate what happens with your assets.

Depending on the size and complexity of your estate, you may also consider a **revocable living trust** in addition to a will. Although a living trust can only provide a base level of protection against potential estate taxes, it will provide more privacy and the ability to greatly reduce or eliminate the complexity and time associated with having to process your estate through probate. A revocable living trust created during your lifetime can hold most of your investments and assets and uses your Social Security number for income tax purposes. The living trust, being revocable, can be amended, and assets can be put in and taken out of the trust at any time prior to your death. Upon your death, the trust becomes a separate legal entity with its own tax identification number managed by the trustee you have named to execute your instructions in the trust document.

A few additional documents deal with your decisions if you are incapacitated or unable to make them on your own. **A durable financial power of attorney** names an individual to make financial decisions on your behalf if you are incapacitated or unable to make them. The same is accomplished for health-care decisions with a **durable health-care power of attorney or proxy.** Without either of these power-of-attorney forms, your family would need to go to court to be appointed as your legal guardian.

In the event that you are permanently unable to make health-care decisions, **a living will** and **advanced medical directive** provide guidance on end-of-life decisions, such as a do-not-resuscitate order. Copies of these forms should be maintained on file with your health-care providers.

By looking at the "soft" and "hard" decisions for your estate plan, a process begins to emerge. This is critical. Most people want to improve their planning, wherever they are today, but frankly they are usually quite stuck. They are not completely sure where to start. So to have a process that communicates a clear beginning, middle, and end is empowering, in and of itself. Let's face it, we all like to know what to expect and what's going to happen next.

When you begin a new relationship of any kind, particularly a new professional relationship, or when you engage someone to do work on your behalf, you want to feel clear and confident about how it will work out. How long will things take? What are the costs? What's the process going to look like? What can you expect? Those are the questions that help to get you launched in the right direction.

To help achieve clarity, begin at the end. What we have found quite interesting about starting with the estate plan—which is beginning with the end in mind—is the estate plan can become a powerful doorway to deeper conversations and planning. Thinking about your life through the lens of your legacy provides you with powerful insights into who you want to become, what more you want to do, and what you want to be remembered for. Not unlike Nobel, when you think critically about these things, you can often tap into areas of significant motivation and energy that can be redirected into the rest of your planning and your life. Most advisors suggest starting with the financial plan, but we prefer tying the financial plan and estate plan together. We intentionally like to start with the estate planning conversation because it provides the clarity you need to make decisions on how to orchestrate your financial plan.

Avoid a nightmare for your heirs—get organized

A big part of the estate planning process, and one that may seem obvious, is getting organized. You can leave a horrendous mess for your loved ones if you don't have your finances organized. If you are married, you could be leaving your spouse with a load of financial concerns and questions at the same time he or she is experiencing the debilitating heartache of loss. To avoid this, we encourage you to imagine that you are organizing your financial life into neat and tidy boxes. It actually can be a little bit therapeutic even, when you start getting organized like this.

Think of it as a tool bench. Have you ever needed to do a job around the house and found your tools jumbled in a pile on the bench from the last time you pulled them out? Or have you been unable to find a tool that got shoved into a drawer? Does that make you feel confident and secure? Of course not. Quite the opposite is how we typically feel in that type of situation. We would much prefer to be able to reliably find what we need when we need it. A tool box, or several of them, can help us accomplish that. Organization makes it a lot easier for us to get the work done in a timely, efficient, and correct way.

It is commonly the case among couples that one spouse takes primary responsibility for the finances. The other spouse, more often than not, is to some degree in the dark and doesn't know completely what they have, where it is, what it is worth, or how it is owned. During a time of loss and mourning, when life feels confusing enough, it can be overwhelming to have to figure out all of the details for the first time.

Organizing your financial life means you care about someone other than yourself. And you are communicating that you don't want your survivors to have to clean up your mess. Getting organized shows your love and regard for whoever that may be—your spouse or other loved ones. It is empowering for you and a blessing for them.

It is similar to the way a couple should be thinking about each other's medications. Unfortunately, a lot of times one spouse doesn't know all the medications and wouldn't know what to tell the first responders or doctors in an emergency. It is sound advice that you should keep a list of the medicines, their strengths, how often you take them, and where they are kept in the house. When it comes to financial and estate planning, your spouse and others whom you will entrust with your financial affairs should know where the important documents are kept and what they include, just in case something happens.

Many advisors have had this experience: A widow comes into the office with a grocery bag full of mail that she has received over the last two months since her husband passed away. She doesn't know what goes to whom or what should be where. We've personally observed the heartbreak when sitting down and sorting through everything in order to help a grieving widow figure it all out. Sometimes, a year or two after a death, an insurance policy or an investment account shows up. Due to the disorganization and lack of shared knowledge, the spouse or family hadn't even realized the policy or investment was there.

Getting organized is essential, as you prepare to do more in the way of creating a more impactful life and a more meaningful legacy. It is a step toward doing right by yourself, your family, and others. With an incomplete financial analysis and your documents in disarray, you can't clearly see where you stand today, let alone how it will impact your loved ones when you're gone. You can't appreciate the big picture if all you can see is some small part of it.

An outside perspective

As you put your plans together, you need to gain an outside perspective. You need an advisor who can help you to see beyond the details and keep you on course with your priorities. A good advisor can help to ensure that you are prepared to keep up with life's challenges and that you don't lose sight of what's truly worthwhile.

To help your loved ones manage your affairs when you are gone, you can take care of the details now. Tabulated binders make it easy to locate records. That is basic advice, but it is all too often ignored. Another option is to maintain records electronically, which cuts down on the amount of paper and makes updating easier. You just need to make sure you keep up with technology so that you don't end up with a

A LESSON FROM THE CORN MAZE
Ron Ware

One autumn day several years ago, my family and I were visiting one of those farms where you can get a taste of country life, with hay rides, apple cider—and an elaborate maze made of corn stalks. This one required you to stop at various stations along the maze and mark your ticket with a hole punch, thereby proving your skill at finding your way. The idea was to see how quickly you could navigate the maze.

What happens with most families is that the kids blast off into the maze and the adults are left poking their way slowly along, lost and confused. No exception here. About 20 minutes after we started, my cell phone rang. It was my 11-year-old daughter, informing me that she had made it through all four stations. I'd managed to find one.

"Where are you?" she asked.

"That's what I'm wondering," I responded. "Where are you?"

"I'm up on the observation deck. It's really cool—you can see the whole picture of the maze from up here!" She could see all the rows and pathways—and all I could see were walls of cornstalks surrounding me.

"Pick up a stalk and wave it," she told me, and I did so. "I see you!" she said—and proceeded to guide me through the maze, turn by turn, station by station, until I had navigated it. Or rather, until she had navigated me. For all I know, I'd never have made it through and found all four stations without her perspective. Or it would have taken me until closing time.

As I reflected on the experience, I realized that what she did for me is exactly the picture of what we do for our clients. We help them look beyond the cornstalks so they can see the big picture. We give them that perspective they usually can't find on their own, and then we help guide them so they can successfully navigate the complexity of their lives and realities to arrive at their chosen destination. We find out where they are, and we help them know where they need to turn. They make it through much more quickly and far less painfully. Could they make it on their own? Perhaps. But it certainly helps to have the perspective of someone who has been there.

format that is no longer accessible. Remember floppy disks? Someday people will be saying, "Remember flash drives?"

You need to plan to update the media on which you are saving information. Some advisors and companies provide services giving you the ability to maintain your important documents and records online in a secure virtual vault which can be accessed from anywhere with an Internet connection.

Your files should include a clear statement of your preferences for your funeral or other arrangements. You also need to discuss those matters with loved ones. If it is never discussed or if your death happens suddenly, your surviving spouse or family members may feel a tremendous amount of uncertainty, even anguish, as they wrestle with what you would have wanted. What type of service? What readings, what music? If you don't let them know in advance, your loved ones may feel tension among themselves, and they could leave out something of importance to you. It is hard to think things through in a time of grief. All your preferences can be written down and stored in a filing system along with all the details of your financial affairs.

You also need to make people aware of where your filing system or electronic records are located. One client made all those arrangements and wrote down all their preferences and then stuck the document in a shoe box in the closet. The family didn't find that shoe box until long after he was buried—and there in the closet were all his final desires, discovered too late to implement.

The lesson: It is not enough to have a good filing system with complete information. Your loved ones need to know where you keep it. Your files should also include a directory of where any other important information might be kept, as well as the names, passwords, and contact information of anyone involved in handling your financial affairs. Your loved ones should have a copy of that directory as well.

A good advisor will work with you in tabulating important documents and other information into binders or files online. You should keep your files somewhere they can be easily found—not in a place where guests will frequent, but in a specific and private location. Then tell your loved ones where to find that information. You should have multiple copies of key documents and account user names and passwords—paper copies as well as electronic ones—in case anything gets lost.

This is especially important in second marriages or in other potentially contentious family situations. One client who knew his father had prepared a new, revised will was unable to locate a copy of it. When he coordinated with his stepmother to review his father's files, he found nothing. In addition, it appeared to him that several files that he remembered from the last time he reviewed the files with his father were now missing. Unfortunately for him and his siblings, who would have benefited from the revised will, no copy could be located.

The value of family meetings

Family meetings are useful for communicating details and making sure everybody is on board and apprised of important information. Some clients are very comfortable with sharing financial information in their plan. Others are not. It seems most people prefer not to share specific details.

A couple may wish to gather with their family, perhaps in a home or in a restaurant, with a few trusted advisors present. When we are involved in family meetings like these, we make sure to know in advance what the client is comfortable about sharing. The general idea is to give the children a sense that their parents have a good plan in place. Our role is to assure the children that we have had the opportunity to hear what their parents are trying to accomplish and that we are working to help them achieve those objectives. We let them know that we want to be a resource to the extended family. Almost universally, the children are grateful to be included, and they feel both respected and more confident, knowing that the situation they will someday need to manage is put together well.

After such meetings, we will no longer be strangers to the children during a later time of need, and they're more likely to trust that we are looking out for their parents' best interests. We have a chance to develop a rapport in advance. Therefore, they're not meeting us for the first time, when they are overwhelmed with concerns, responsibilities, and grief. This is a significant and valuable role your advisor can play in supporting your family and the continuity of your legacy.

Reflecting on what you would like to be said about you and what you would like to be remembered for can be a helpful starting point in determining a path for your life and your estate planning. Once you have decided how you would like to be remembered, it is important to take action to put all of your documents and details in place. Don't let your family's last memory of you be a disorganized, relationship-destroying mess. Make sure your estate plan includes the appropriate documents. Express your intentions and wishes to your family. Consider the value of a family meeting to ensure your intentions are known. When the time comes, your family members will be grateful for all that you have done, what you will be remembered for, and for the legacy you will be leaving.

"What you leave behind is not what is engraved in stone monuments, but what is woven into the lives of others."

—PERICLES, Greek statesman, 495 BCE–429 BCE

Chapter Seven

DEATH AND TAXES, OR FAMILY LEGACY?

It is just a cookbook, but it is the favorite possession of one of our clients. Her mother left it to her, and she treasures it. One of the things that makes it so special is that her mother wrote notes and comments in the margins. Today, when our client pulls out that cookbook and sees her mother's handwriting, she feels as if her mother is there in the kitchen with her, sharing tips as they prepare something special together. The memories come pouring back.

By giving her that cookbook, her mother left her a small inheritance of true wealth. True wealth involves the things that money can't buy and death can't take away. Just as it is important to carefully plan how to pass on your financial wealth, we must carefully consider how we wish to pass on our true wealth to future generations.

Passing on our values and stories

One way to do this is through a spiritual or ethical will. This is not a legal document, but a personal message that expresses your wisdom, values, and/or experiences to future generations. The first written ethical wills date back to the 12th century, when Jewish fathers wrote to their sons on how to live an ethical life. These writings were an obligation as a parent, and included both practical advice and timeless words of wisdom—"Don't quarrel, don't oppress others in money or word, instruct your children as I have instructed you."

With a growing awareness that a legacy is far more than material goods or financial assets, ethical wills can be part family history, part love letter, and part self-reflective exercise. Traditional wills involve what you want your loved ones to have; ethical wills involve what you want them to know.

A nonbinding document that should complement traditional legal estate planning documents, an ethical will is by its nature a "spiritual" exercise. An ethical will can be applied in almost any family context when one generation wants to ask, and answer, the big questions: What have I been about? Who were the most influential people in my life? What is the greatest lesson I've ever learned—and want to pass on? Whose forgiveness do I need—and who needs mine? Also, an ethical will is a priceless opportunity to create the personal context for your financial will as a loving expression that gives meaning to the values associated with financial assets—values we want the generations that follow us to know and embrace.

Most often written for children, grandchildren, or unborn heirs by one person or by a couple, an ethical will can be as simple as a one-page "love letter" or can be an audio or video recording. Many people create an ethical will at certain life transition points or to mark an occasion—a golden wedding anniversary, an 80th birthday, a child's college graduation—but it should be regularly revisited. Beyond its benefit as an exercise in self-reflection, an ethical will can be used by parents or grandparents to open a discussion on the other estate planning documents, or illustrate what is in their hearts to help heirs better understand their values about money. Even adult children need a comprehensive discussion of the will, trusts, and philanthropic vehicles in order to understand their parents' intent.

It is important that the language in an ethical will be affirming—even if the intent is to communicate to a child why he or she may not be granted access to assets or allowed to make decisions on them. It can also include a parent's acknowledgment of mistakes. As important as the values and meaning in an ethical will are to the family's history and heritage, grandparents often fret over sounding as if they're lecturing when they want to discuss their values with grandchildren. An ethical will is a way to personally and naturally get points across about where a family came from and where it wants to go—significantly broadening the definition of a family's true wealth.

Little things can make a huge impact in passing on our legacy and how future generations will remember us. Handwritten notes have long been a particularly endearing way to put one's personal stamp on memories. However, in this age of e-mail and texts and tweets, some schools are no longer teaching cursive handwriting because typing has become so pervasive. The personal handwritten note seems destined to become a lost art.

Yet many still perceive a letter in handwriting as coming from somewhere closer to the heart, more powerful and permanent than a printout could ever be. Pen and paper seem the perfect medium for a spiritual will. In the words of the poet Omar Khayyam: "The moving finger writes; and having writ / moves on: nor all your piety and wit / shall lure it back to cancel half a line, / nor all your tears wash out a word of it."

In the book *Letters from Posterity*, historian and author David McCullough collected the words that famous historical American figures wrote to their children. Often, they wrote them from the battlefield, or from places that were many days of travel away from their loved ones. The letters are poignant in the values they communicate and the lessons they teach. From far away, they convey great intimacy.

This is what you can do for your family and for posterity. Money is a big part of what we will leave, but there is much more that we can pass on. We can communicate our values in our own handwriting, so that our great-grandchildren can see the flourishes and quirks of our script, and perhaps our personality. It is a simple but valuable opportunity to put our stamp on what we have learned about life and preserve it for posterity.

Through technology, we also can easily leave the spoken word, either through audio recordings or through video. A relatively inexpensive camera can produce high definition video. It doesn't have to be anything fancy, but there can also be tremendous value in the recording, whether it is just telling a story or telling a little bit about our own life and experiences and the values that we hold in our heart.

There are so many things that people can do to keep their voice, face, and expressions alive for generations to come. A client's father was the pilot for Air Force One while John F. Kennedy was president. One evening that client was surfing the web and came across a video of a Florida news report of his father's funeral at Arlington Cemetery. Somebody had posted it on a website, but he couldn't figure out how to access the video. We helped that client by tracking down the television station that aired the video; we got a copy of it, burned it onto a CD, and gave it to him on a flash drive as well. The piece that was produced by the newscast talked about his father's life and how he had served his country by flying Air Force One. What a wonderful story—and what a great keepsake for the family.

Our parents used to cut out clippings from the newspaper. In this day and age, you can do so much more. You can use the services offered by a variety of companies which produce keepsake albums that tell your family's story. Let's face it, in everybody's life there's a story—something significant and substantial that needs to be preserved for generations. These will be stories that our children's children will tell their children.

Passing on your money

Another way that you can communicate and pass on your values is through your choice of charities to which you give financial support. The record of your life will show what you felt was important as you passed through this world. In leaving money for charitable purpose and specific organizations, you are endorsing the values which that charity is trying to promote or the impact it is trying to make.

The nature of families' wealth varies widely, as do the methods for distributing it to beneficiaries. People make outright bequests or set up trusts to benefit generations to come—or they can engage in a family controlled charity.

Family foundations and donor-advised funds are two of the most popular family-led organizations that can be set up. A family foundation is a fully functional, not-for-profit entity that is controlled by and receives most of its funding from a single individual, family, or business. It is a way for you and your family to strengthen your community, assist those in need, protect the environment, or create some other meaningful difference in the world. By establishing a family foundation, you are able to exercise complete control over how funds are invested and distributed to support various causes and institutions that you care about, while creating an organization that will be a lasting legacy to carry on your family or business name.

Unlike a family foundation, a donor-advised fund is established within a not-for-profit charity that administers the fund and controls the investment decisions. The contributor is then able to make grant recommendations to the charity on the disbursement of the funds. A donor-advised fund also can be established through a local community foundation, an independent foundation, or various financial institutions.

Donor-advised funds are clearly the most inexpensive way to accomplish your philanthropic goals via a family-led charity. You will not be facing a significant funding level or minimum threshold, and administration costs and complexity are low.

Family foundations are generally for more sizable contributions, with a minimum of $250,000 to $1 million. There's a lot involved in a family foundation, including regulation and governance issues; to justify doing it, you need an appropriate level of wealth. Organizations such as Foundation Source (www.foundationsource.com) can streamline the administration of your foundation and generally will tell you that $250,000 is a minimum level to begin with if you use them as a resource.

Often when we show clients a plan that includes contributions to charity, they will presume that those contributions will no longer be part of the family wealth. But in fact, it is still family wealth—with a very distinct characteristic. Ideally, one or more of your family members would be able to become involved as a board member, if you create your own foundation. Or, if you have a donor-advised fund, your family members could serve in an advisory role to help direct where the money will go, how it will have the greatest impact, and to monitor the fund on a periodic basis. Even if the financial wealth is not passed directly to the family, the involvement of family members in the continual administration of the family's philanthropy will pass on the core values of giving and gratitude.

For some higher-wealth holders in the United States, family offices have become popular because they are useful to the entire family, including multiple generations within such families. They are designed to help families coordinate and administer family trusts for generations to come. As more and more descendants—and potential beneficiaries—enter the equation, there is more and more to coordinate and administer. The continuing interaction of family members involved in a trust can become what we call a dynastic trust arrangement, spanning multiple generations in some cases.

The wealth that you earmark for social and charitable purposes can give the younger members of your family in the generations ahead the opportunity to become involved in your philanthropy and to consider giving life to their own charitable interest—a noble pursuit that they otherwise might not have experienced. The management of your wealth gives them an opening to become involved in good causes. Ideally, you will get your family involved before you pass away—you shouldn't just set up a fund that gets turned over upon your death.

This can be a tremendous opportunity for parents or grandparents to share their values with their family, now and in the future. The children may not necessarily want to go in the same charitable direction, but opening that communication is essential to learning about the passions of both generations and offering the children the financial means to pursue them. The likely result will be a blend of the charitable interests of all the generations involved. This works best when you can function as a team, pursuing those interests with a shared sense of ownership.

If you can draft your family into such a relationship before your death, philanthropy will become a continuation of something you started together. It won't feel to your heirs as if it is something that has been thrust upon them, and it becomes far less likely that a child will abandon his parents' or grandparents' causes because he or she doesn't agree with them philosophically or politically.

The assets that matter

Certainly, then, money matters. The reason you may decide to move in the direction of philanthropic giving is that your net worth, as well as your tax and financial projections, open the possibilities for your personal true wealth—the most valuable of your assets—that may be at work within your heart. This is what you will have the chance to pass on for posterity. Money does indeed talk, but it is the heart that listens, discerns, and decides what is best to talk about.

PART THREE:

ACTING DIFFERENTLY

"What this power is I cannot say; all I know is that it exists and it becomes available only when a man is in that state of mind in which he knows exactly what he wants and is fully determined not to quit until he finds it."

—ALEXANDER GRAHAM BELL, Scottish inventor, 1847–1922

Chapter Eight

DISCOVERY: WHAT YOU WANT

R on Ware tells the following story about an initial meeting with potential clients.

Tom and Nancy came into our office for an assessment and a second opinion. They were hoping to take their financial and estate planning to the next level and were seeking our advice. We had been recommended to them, which is most often how we meet new individuals and families. This couple was concerned about their existing advisor and questioned whether that advisor was really managing their various financial details and providing for their future in the best possible way.

Tom was a man's man, big, burly, and a genuine tough guy. As our meeting started, he was silent at first. A Vietnam veteran, he had subsequently served as a police officer for years but retired on disability after taking a crowbar to the eye. Nancy was a company executive—and it was clear that they had come at her urging. Tom didn't speak. It was as if he had nothing to say.

I spoke with the couple briefly about broad topics, including Vietnam. "Before anything," I said, touching Tom's arm, "I want to thank you. Thank you for your service. How have you been doing all these years since the war? I know it wasn't easy for so many of you."

The husband looked at me almost in disbelief, a tear on his cheek.

"I'm sorry," I said. "I hope I wasn't out of line there."

"No, no, not at all," Tom said. "You don't understand—nobody asks that question. Thank you."

And the silent man began to talk. He talked about his experiences in Vietnam. He talked about his work on the police force back in the States. He said that in talking to veterans returning from Iraq and Afghanistan, he had felt a tremendous sense of healing because he had been in their shoes. He served in the infantry in Vietnam and had seen too much—things that took years to overcome.

"Talking to these kids coming back now," he said, "and sharing what I went through and how I coped—well, it's like I can minister to them or something. They're feeling post-traumatic stress, and I have so much I can say to help them. It's been the best thing I have ever done in my life."

Tom was letting down his defenses and letting his emotions out. I was seeing, so very clearly, what Tom cared about—and the cause that he well might choose to continue supporting.

Do you suppose this would have played out differently if I had leaned back in my chair and asked, while still perusing the couple's data, "So, now, let me see here, what are your goals?"

Beyond the sheer insensitivity, this approach sidesteps the kind of heartfelt interaction an advisor should have with you. Neither an advisor nor you can know what you are interested in or how to get there until you have identified the things you care about most and want to support financially. These things usually consist of life, people, and purposes—or as we like to say for short: more living and more giving.

Uncovering what you really care about

When it comes to money or financial wealth, many people eventually get to a point in life when they begin to acknowledge that they have more than enough wealth for their personal and family needs. Then they can start to open themselves up to the idea of sharing some of their wealth. Others, however, are just stuck—feeling unclear as to what extent they will be able to provide for their family or unsure if they will have the money they'll need during retirement.

In both individual and family wealth situations, people may find they have a desire to give back and make a difference. They want to contribute philanthropically or charitably. Some people are not certain they can afford to give, and many are not even sure where to start, since they often have little past experience along these lines to guide them. They need to find ways, tools, and resources to help them begin to get in touch with what they really care about—their passions.

The newspaper review

Here's an exercise that can be very instructive: Sit down over the weekend with your cup of coffee, a newspaper, and three different color markers or highlighters. Read through the newspaper once with one marker and circle everything that makes you sad. Then go through the paper again and circle, in a different color, whatever makes you angry. Then use a different color for what makes you joyful. When you are done, take an inventory of the news stories that you have circled or highlighted in each of the colors and categories.

Sadness clearly connects us with passion because it reflects our empathy and caring about a situation. Anger and indignation indicate a drive to do something about the wrongs in this world. And joy can be a wellspring for our life.

Two of the most powerful emotions that we express are love and hate. What is it that you love or makes you joyful? What is it that makes you sad or angry, that you hate? By examining these two fundamental feelings and what stirs them up in our lives, we can start to determine where our purpose and passion lies.

We should give far more attention to what these categories mean for each of us individually, rather than to the many other things we focus on routinely. This is just a beginning to help us understand what we really care about. And for most of us, our caring extends beyond just ourselves and our families. This exercise can serve as an invaluable tool to help us discover our points of passion and joy, in order to form a clearer vision for our life and our legacy. For some of us, it can become the foundation of a family mission statement, which can be very useful in designing and refining plans for our wealth and other important decisions as we move forward.

Telling your story

One of the best ways to articulate your values and the things you care about is to examine and explore your personal and family stories. This can be a tremendous opportunity for revelation and discovery. We suggest you discuss this with an experienced advisor in life and legacy planning who can provide you with guidance, a different perspective, and raise additional questions or provide you with insights that you may overlook. You may also choose to do this on your own during a time of reflection and journaling. If you do this on your own, make sure to allow yourself some time in between reflections or journal writings to contemplate your previous thoughts and writings.

Ask and answer questions around subjects like these (to the extent they apply to you):

- your childhood
- your parents
- your most joyful and painful memories of those years

- the work ethic and values your parents taught and modeled for you (both positive and negative)
- your parents' marriage
- your grade school, secondary school, college, and vocational experiences
- how you met your spouse
- becoming and learning to be a parent
- helping aging parents and/or siblings
- your developed and matured perspectives in faith, history, business, politics, and the world
- experiences that made an impact or changed your life

As you explore the terrain of your personal family story, you will begin to uncover your values, beliefs, ethics, morals, and hoped-for outcomes for the future for yourself and others.

By examining your family story and what you have experienced and have been taught about money, you can start to understand some of your attitudes and habits related to your wealth. Wealth is about so much more than money. And there are so many subtle aspects about your relationship with money that affect your sense of wholeness, wellness, and ultimately, your vision for the future.

You may be smart, successful, and driven, but you still may not have stopped to smell the roses long enough to know what it is you really care about most. Some people can find this conversation uncomfortable or too "crunchy granola" for their liking. If this is you, we urge you to press through this discomfort. You will not regret doing so. This can be a crucial step toward getting in touch with something more important and more motivating than money.

Describing your journey can be quite powerful and illuminating—for you and for those you care about. Getting a chance to talk and share your story out loud with someone who is an effective listener is particularly valuable as you embark on this quest to really discover what it is you want.

Getting down to core values

Once your family stories and values begin to surface, it is important to document them. With our clients' permission, we may occasionally audio record their stories and then have the stories transcribed and produced in writing to assist them in concretizing their ideas. The next step based on your stories will be to craft a personalized set of core values. Whether you work with an advisor or do this on your own, extract a list of values from your stories and then refine it until you have a list of your core values. Then sit down and review it. We review the core values together with our clients. We ask them: "What are your thoughts about the list? Is there anything you would add or remove?" When you see your values written on paper, it usually generates an added sense of direction and enthusiasm for pursuing goals that embody those values.

After determining your core values, ask yourself: "What have I done and what do I think about that I might want to do to make sure that I am supporting and living out these values that I have expressed? Is there anything I might consider doing differently?"

It is our experience that it is during this step when people start talking about certain things they are not doing now that they wish they were, and wondering aloud whether there is any way that they could do them. This is a huge pivotal point in the planning process, because they are thinking of pursuing something they care about now and are no longer willing to just idly sit by and accept the status quo.

The conversation about your family story leads to your core values, which then enables you and your advisor to begin working out how you can put your values into action most effectively with the greatest impact. The advisor's role is not only to assist you in gaining clarity about your legacy and perhaps even the beginning of a philanthropic vision, but also to take a close look at where you are now. This approach will clarify your view about what obstacles might seem to be in the way and help you to begin thinking creatively about how you can navigate around them so that you can reach your destination.

The discovery of what you want to do and what you wish to support must come first. Hopefully it is accompanied with the sure knowledge that, yes, it is possible to support one or more worthwhile causes without sacrificing your family's immediate well-being. Then, with a direction in mind, you can identify just where you are starting from and what specifically you can do to ensure the smoothest journey toward your "more that matters."

In our practice, this creates what we call our Life & Legacy Plan Design Book. It effectively becomes the map and directions—which then allows our clients to put their foot on the gas pedal with a clear path to travel.

How much is enough to leave my heirs?

While discussing what you want, it is important to also look at what you want for your children or family members. If you feel that Warren Buffett has earned some credibility on financial matters, then you might want to heed his advice: Parents should leave their children enough money so they could do anything, but not so much that they could do nothing.

Most of us who are parents want our children to have a better life than we had growing up. Even if we didn't struggle, there is always room to improve their situation. But does there reach a point where what we might financially leave our children becomes too much? How much is too much?

Another important question: How are you going to go about leaving your property and assets to your children and heirs? It is not hard to see that a distribution that could be quite beneficial to one individual could be detrimental and destructive to another, even within the same family. Many parents tell themselves, "I'm just going to leave it equally to my children after both of us have passed away, and they can receive their shares outright."

That is clearly the default plan for handling most families' estates. But it is an extremely limited and possibly harmful approach since it is not based on each child's capability or individual situation. Both of these questions must be considered carefully: "How much should we leave to the children and heirs?" and "What's the best way to pass it on to them?"

And there is one more critical question: "Why?" Many estate planners and advisors work with clients for years without ever delving into this foundational question that they really should be asking first.

Obviously it is good and natural for all of us to instinctively want to leave our wealth to our children. After all, our children are the most tangible manifestation of our legacy, and "charity begins at home," right? But don't overlook the fundamental question of why you are doing so. Asking the "why" question demonstrates responsibility, stewardship, and love. "What is it that I am trying to promote? What values, what outcomes, what results am I hoping to create?"

Our clients find it refreshing and even freeing to consider these questions and come up with personal answers to them. Such close examination is bound to help you clarify and promote your true objectives. It is much more intentional and thoughtful than the aimless default of "everything equally to my kids."

Where do you draw that line between encouraging your children and heirs to live productive lives and robbing them of a work ethic and the virtues associated with at least some experience facing challenges and struggle?

Parents are the ones who know their children best and need to weigh such matters: How much should John get? Should Mary really get the same amount? Should they get the money in the same form? Who needs it more? Who is likely to use it more wisely?

The reason that parents often prefer an equal distribution to each child is that they want to communicate an equal measure of love and not favor one over another. The reality, however, is that one or more of the children or heirs may have genuinely legitimate needs, while another may be doing exceedingly well. Perhaps that child is even telling Mom and Dad not to leave them money because doing so would further complicate his or her own tax issues.

Think about your children and heirs as individuals. What's good for one may not be good for another. Is one more of a spendthrift, or is one more at risk of losing part of your family wealth in a divorce? You will want to be sensitive to these issues when deciding how to leave money to each child or person. If you take a purposeful approach and ask yourself what you are trying to accomplish, it is likely to become clearer to you how much is appropriate to leave for each.

It's not that all children who inherit wealth do not know how to properly handle it, but there are numerous famous poster children for poorly planned inheritances. In these situations, the inherited wealth has usually meant the person has never had to really work or secure gainful employment. This is usually a contradiction and a negative contrast when juxtaposed against the family's reputation and history during their lifetime. You can be fairly certain that these families would have done things differently had they known that their family trusts were going to support and even promote a sometimes out-of-control, lazy, and even party lifestyle. Too much wealth can cause harm. It can be a curse rather than a blessing. And how the money is distributed plays a key role.

You certainly have the flexibility to create and develop a distribution method that is appropriate for each of your heirs. Trust funds can be structured in many ways and can be very useful in providing for the distribution of inheritances. Many individuals have tied distributions from a trust to whether the child attains certain milestones in life—college graduation, perhaps, or buying a house. More commonly, distributions are tied to the recipient's age rather than to actual events. An important thing to consider is the recipient's level of maturity, rather than strictly what he or she has accomplished. What ability has the child shown for handling finances wisely? How much regard does he or she show for others?

In Jim Stovall's novel *The Ultimate Gift*, a billionaire's will assigns 12 tasks to his playboy nephew as conditions for further inheritance. Those tasks, or "gifts," involve such core values as working hard, developing friendships, facing problems, learning, dreaming, loving, laughing, and giving. For example, to learn the value of hard work, the nephew is asked to spend a month digging post holes at the Texas ranch of one of the billionaire's friends. By the end of the month, the nephew has come to appreciate the importance of hard work and the diligence in lining up and digging the holes properly the first time. This task assignment is an example of a creative and worthwhile approach that may inspire you to develop such trust provisions of your own.

Another reason a trust makes sense is that you can structure it to protect beneficiaries from a whole array of future risks, including creditors, lawsuits, and divorcing spouses. Generally speaking, if your children or grandchildren inherit money through a trust, so long as the right attributes and provisions are drafted into the trust and they retain the property in trust, it will be protected from creditors, divorce, and other risks. The use of a trust in your planning can protect your intentions and make sure your goals for your wealth are properly executed.

Write down your goals

Once you have determined your core values and started to develop an overall vision, it is wise to put pen to paper or fingers to keyboard and write a list of your life goals. By doing so, you engage a different part of your mind than when you just think about them. You will feel a greater commitment once you have put something on paper. Your hopes and dreams become somehow more visible and tangible. They become something that you will strive to accomplish, rather than something you are idly thinking about.

Writing down your goals, keeping them with your important papers so that your executor and trustees can see them, and sharing them with your spouse and other loved ones—perhaps even having family meetings to discuss them—is important. This will go a long way toward helping everyone focus on just what you want to accomplish with your wealth and the contributions you wish to make to the world.

It is all part of developing and solidifying your overall vision. You may have a wide variety of things you want to accomplish, so it is important to prioritize your goals and decide which ones you will develop more specifically. Writing them down also makes it easier for you to review your progress on a regular basis. Any process requires review and reflection as life circumstances change. Your priorities, passions, and even your values can change over time. When you have your goals in writing, you can easily see when it might be appropriate to review and revise them.

Discovering your passions and examining your stories to discover your core values provide you with the foundation for your planning. It is from this process and examination of why and how you might want to leave assets to your family that you can then focus on your goals. Just as in planning a trip or vacation, the first step is to determine a destination. Without a defined destination, any road will get you there. Once you more fully understand where you want to go, it's time to begin the process of holistically assessing your resources, relationships, business interests, and all other elements that a truly comprehensive approach implies.

"Do what you can, with what you have, where you are."

—**THEODORE ROOSEVELT,** 26th U.S. president, 1858–1919

Chapter Nine

ANALYSIS: WHAT YOU HAVE

Y ou no doubt have heard the instructions about how to use an oxygen mask when you are aboard an airplane.

"Should the cabin experience a sudden loss of pressure, oxygen masks will drop down from above your seat. To start the flow of oxygen, pull the mask towards you. Place it firmly over your nose and mouth, secure the elastic band behind your head, and breathe normally. Although the bag does not inflate, oxygen is flowing to the mask. If you are traveling with a child or someone who needs assistance, secure your mask first, and then assist the other person."

Putting your own mask on first, before helping others, might seem a rather selfish course of action. But the rationale becomes obvious: You cannot be of any service to anyone if you are lying unconscious on the floor for lack of oxygen. Likewise, if you haven't taken care of your own financial needs first, you will be unable to reach out to help others. You have to be able to make sure that you are providing for yourself before you can do anything beyond that. It is this thought process that led to the development of The Planning Pyramid.

The Planning Pyramid

As you think about doing more that matters and creating a plan to live more and give more, it can be helpful to see the process as a Planning Pyramid. (See the diagram below.)

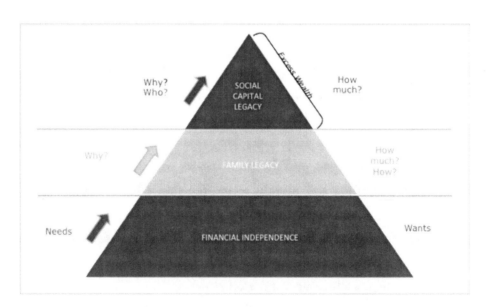

The Planning Pyramid's three tiers show how a family legacy and philanthropy can be built only upon a secure financial base.

The pyramid's three tiers show how a family legacy and then a social capital legacy can only be created in proper sequence—and only after first assuring yourself that you have what you need financially. In this illustration, progress in taking your family's planning to the next level is like ascending a pyramid. As you take your planning to the next level and up the pyramid, your values lead you to specific goals and actions.

The base of the pyramid constitutes "financial independence." This is the nuts and bolts of your financial life. If you can't take care of yourself, you obviously can't begin to think about taking care of others. Until you have confidence that your plan provides sufficient resources to support your needs and wants throughout your lifetime, it is difficult to progress in any meaningful way to higher levels of planning.

Once you have established in your mind that the financial base is solid, you can then begin to work more seriously on creating an impactful family legacy. With a greater focus on the family legacy you hope to create, you must decide why you want to leave your family an inheritance and how much of your wealth would be an appropriate and adequate funding amount for this purpose. It is not enough just to minimize taxes and maximize wealth to your heirs. A responsible legacy creates alignment with your values and leaves you confident that your financial legacy, as it pertains to your family in particular, will be helpful and not hurtful.

The pinnacle of the pyramid is your social capital legacy, or philanthropy. It is a level of planning that the vast majority of people never get to, not because they wouldn't have liked to get there, but because most people do not have a plan that leaves them sufficiently confident in their own financial independence and their ability to create their desired family legacy. As we have shared previously, gifts to charitable causes or organizations need not come at the expense of your own financial needs or providing for your family. And with the right kind of planning and expertise, you can multiply your excess wealth so that, in many cases, your ability to financially support the causes and organizations you care about can be increased substantially. You have control over who will benefit from your excess wealth and how.

Do we really have enough to do more?

The first step in establishing the foundation of your Planning Pyramid and determining your financial independence is to determine your net worth. Your net worth is equal to the sum of all of your assets minus any liabilities or debt. Once you have a good grasp on your net worth, it is important to get a clear understanding of what your income and expenses are. Understanding your sources of income, and the amount of additional income that will be necessary each year from your assets to cover your annual expenses, will help you gain a sense of self-confidence about your own well-being and your ability to sustain yourself over the long haul, on your terms. With that confidence, you can finally give yourself the permission to do more for your family and beyond.

We recently sat with a couple who were convinced that doing more was not something that was possible for them. In fact, they were reluctant to even articulate their dreams. "Those things will never happen," the couple said. Our response was, in effect: "Let's test your theory. Let's examine your finances and run a stress test to see if they would hold up if you tried doing more. You may be right, or you may be wrong."

And, in fact, they were wrong. After a series of meetings, in which it became progressively clear that this couple had much to contribute, it was gratifying to see them looking at each other, almost dumbstruck, as if to say, "Did you ever think this was possible?" For years, they had convinced themselves that they had an impossible dream—and now they had discovered a new level of freedom to pursue their wishes to give back more substantially.

As you begin analyzing your own situation more completely and planning better, determining what you have, need, and want is very helpful. This may seem obvious, but what is not so obvious is how to allow yourself to think and dream big enough.

Jim Collins, author of *Good to Great*, coined the phrase "Big Hairy Audacious Goal." If you are like most of our clients and are inherently thrifty, this is easier said than done. But when it comes to assessing what you really want, this is no time to think small.

This is your chance to establish your own personal "bucket list" if you will. And, as you go about creating this (doing so together is recommended for married couples), think about places and things that you have always wanted to experience. What brings you joy, peace, fulfillment, and even perhaps a bit of exhilaration? Write these ideas down and estimate conservatively what it would cost to accomplish them.

As you develop this next level of thinking within your plan, after you have established your personal dream sheet, it is time to think more about your family legacy.

Do you know your children and perhaps grandchildren well enough to know what some of their heartfelt desires are? Which of these dreams would you like to make come true? If getting this specific isn't possible, what big areas or core values within your family legacy would you like to be certain you fund well? Remember, aimless inheritances do not equal a family legacy. Be thoughtful, careful, and intentional about how you allocate your wealth to your children and future generations.

Whether specific or more general, do some figuring and estimate what all of this will cost, as well as the most likely timing of these expenses. Which of your family legacy goals and objectives do you want to make happen during your lifetime? Which ones are best funded after your death?

Taking the time to think big, and doing this well, will leave you feeling energized and expectant about the future. It also will facilitate a heightened level of confidence about your financial independence and family legacy, at least in terms of understanding what you desire. After you see this side of the equation more clearly, you can now turn to assessing what you have. Because what you have is only really relevant in relationship to what you need and what you want.

We have long been amazed at how frequently we see smart, successful families who are unwittingly stuck in a place of uncertainty about their future, or worse yet, a place of unspoken anxiety and fear. This is primarily due to not articulating their needs and wants well enough. When people do this analysis and then consider what they have, these numbers can be compared on a projected basis out to life expectancy. This is when individuals really start to feel a sense of freedom. One of the great antidotes to fear is freedom. Isn't that where you want to be?

Try not to be someone who is voluntarily and unnecessarily holding back. Spell it all out with the help of planning specialists who have your best interest in mind. Think bigger and plan better. Your life and your legacy hang in the balance. And if you are ever going to truly believe that you actually do have excess wealth and can do more, this kind of detailed and specific "dreaming" on behalf of yourself and your loved ones is the only way that you can reasonably expect to get there.

What happens under your current estate plan?

When we explain that the three potential beneficiaries of an estate are family, charity, and the government, most people will say they would prefer to leave as little as possible to that last one. What most people do not realize is that with proper planning, you can choose the first two and send the tax man packing.

The next question to ask is this: "In your current estate plan, do you know how much, or what percentage, of your money will go to each of these three potential beneficiaries?"

Many people don't know the answer and feel frustrated. As stewards of the resources and assets with which we have been blessed, we need to know what will become of them upon our death. If we don't know, it is time to get some answers.

Even if you have done traditional estate planning, it may not hold up as you originally envisioned. Many people believe they are covered because they created an estate plan within the past few years and feel that it is pretty current. But just because a plan is current does not necessarily mean that it is adequate or that it will eliminate potential estate taxes. Traditional estate planning is not necessarily zero estate-tax planning.

Families who have done traditional estate planning, and who have a taxable estate, will often subject the heirs and the family to estate tax liability, often acquiring life insurance to pay the taxes. But for about the last 100 years or so, the most successful and well-prepared families have not paid federal estate taxes. Instead they leave a lot of money to charity, while increasing the amount left to their family and heirs. This is a win-win situation.

We think creating a zero estate-tax plan through charitable planning is a critical area for families to evaluate. Even those who initially are not particularly philanthropy-minded will often develop that charitable heartbeat when they better understand what happens to their money under their current estate plan—and then compare that with how it could be with charitable giving in place.

Do you have excess wealth?

After taking a comprehensive look at your financial affairs, you may reach the conclusion that you are able to meet your income needs and wants, and that, in fact, you are on track to have more than enough to pursue the various dreams and goals that you have outlined for yourself and your loved ones. You have hopefully also made provisions to meet whatever various contingencies could occur in the future and manage whatever risks you may need to protect yourself from, including long-term custodial care and the risk of inflation. Then, and only then, will you feel reassured—clear and confident. And that is the point when you can ask yourself a very important question: Do you have excess wealth?

As we have shared with you throughout this book, most people, of course, initially don't believe they do. But those who discover that they have excess wealth begin to feel an enhanced freedom to reach out. Time and again we have observed how a whole new world, of possibilities and dreams to contribute and give back and to build a meaningful legacy, opens to them impactful goals that had not even been on their list before. What is missing from your list? You have achieved so much, now harness all that you have used to build financial wealth to build a legacy.

*"Our eyes only see and our ears only hear
what our brain is looking for."*

—DAN SULLIVAN, founder and president of Strategic Coach, Inc.

Chapter Ten

DESIGN: WHAT YOU CAN DO

O nce you have confidently acknowledged that you are in fact blessed with resources beyond what you personally need, what now?

Having helped others to see this for the last 20 years, we have come to appreciate that there really are only two things you can do at this point—live more and give more! Both can be incredibly joyful, but they are also two very distinct actions. Finding a way to do both is what we have found works best. Our hopes for you are the same as they are for all of our clients—that you ultimately discover that you do have excess wealth and then boldly act on this newfound realization. With this discovery comes the freedom to improve your life and the lives of others.

In many ways, the sky is the limit in terms of what you can do with your excess wealth. However, too many of us who have long dreamt about our golden retirement years haven't been honest with ourselves. One of the definitions of the word *retirement* in Webster's Dictionary is "to be put out of use." Sounds exciting, golden even, doesn't it? Hardly!

We have a wealth of experience in working with retirees. Having advised many former entrepreneurs, executives, professionals, and other hard-working, creative, self-made millionaires, we have found that not one of these folks has been willing to accept a traditional definition of retirement.

We think you will find that you can travel, golf, garden, or engage in a favorite hobby only so much. For those we have served over the years, their so-called retirement is "golden" because it becomes their finest season, closing chapter, or crescendo. It is their highest platform and opportunity to serve—a time when they continue to give of themselves to create value, give help, and to counsel others. While they give of their money, they also give from their deep well of relationships, resources, skills, and personal passions.

When it comes to what you *can* do, we have found that for our clients who discover they have excess wealth, creating a plan to utilize and maximize it for the benefit of their family and others quickly becomes a matter of what they *must* do. This isn't some kind of obligatory involvement. It is about leadership, responsibility, and selflessness. The opportunities abound. The needs are vast. Perhaps you are aware of the vacuum of leadership, marketplace savvy, strategic thinking, and wise counsel—the plain need for executive-level help—

that exists in the social sector. The need is great in many charitable and nonprofit organizations, churches, and other faith communities, foundations, and yet-unformed social enterprises (which people like you may be led to create).

Here are some examples of planning you may want to consider in doing more that matters.

Creating a simple planned gift

Most people leave money to their family through beneficiary designations as well as by naming beneficiaries in their estate documents. And commonly, when families decide to leave wealth to one or more charitable organizations, they presume that these organizations should simply be included as beneficiaries in their will or trust. But that may not be the most tax-efficient way of managing this.

A planned gift is simply a gift of some of your property that is left to charity through provisions within your estate plan. Perhaps one of the simplest and most income-tax-efficient means of implementing this is to consider designating a portion of your retirement plan as a planned gift.

Let's say you have $500,000 in an investment account that you have already paid income tax on, such as stock or real estate, and another $500,000 in a qualified retirement account, like an IRA, 401(k), or 403(b). When looking at the most income-tax-efficient way of leaving assets to your children or family members, the investment account would be the most tax efficient because these investments were made with after-tax dollars. Therefore, your heirs will receive these assets without having to pay any income tax.

Your heirs will get an additional advantage if they decide to sell the after-tax assets usually by qualifying for a step-up in the cost basis of the assets at your death. Generally, the cost basis of an investment is the original purchase price plus any additions, such as reinvested dividends or capital improvements to a home. Under the current tax law, the cost basis of an after-tax asset will step up to the market value of the asset on the date of your death. This will potentially reduce or eliminate any taxable gain to your beneficiaries when they decide to sell the asset. For example, if you were to sell a stock for $100,000 that you originally purchased over a year ago for $40,000, you would have a capital gain of $60,000 that could be subject to capital gains tax (the market value of $100,000 minus the cost basis of $40,000). If you passed away before you sold the stock, the stock beneficiaries would get a step-up in the cost basis of the stock from $40,000 to $100,000. Therefore, if the beneficiaries sold the stock, there would not be a capital gain to be taxable to the beneficiaries due to the market value equaling the new cost basis.

On the other hand, if you were to leave your beneficiaries the qualified retirement account, they would have to pay the deferred income tax on the entire account, which may be at higher ordinary income tax rates. However, if you leave some portion or all of that retirement account to a charity or nonprofit organization, it pays no income tax due to its tax-exempt status.

Therefore, when we look at after-tax investments and qualified retirement accounts, you and your beneficiaries are usually better off by leaving the after-tax assets to your heirs. Unfortunately, people typically just include charitable beneficiaries in their will and name family members as beneficiaries of retirement accounts. This is backward. The more tax-efficient, after-tax assets should be left to the family and the taxable retirement account should be left to the tax-exempt nonprofit organization.

Real-life examples of what is possible

Let's share a few situations that we have been involved with, in the hopes of painting a clearer picture for you of what is possible.

Jim and Mary—more income while giving more to family and charity

Jim and Mary retired in 2012 at age 62. A combination of their pensions, Social Security, interest, and dividends would provide them with $121,000 of income each year. They owned a $600,000 home free of mortgage, a $750,000 piece of investment real estate, a $500,000 investment portfolio, and Jim had $700,000 in an IRA. They gave $12,000 per year to their favorite charities and planned to withdraw $21,000 each year from Jim's IRA to supplement their income. Their twin adult children were 35. They were very proud of their kids and hoped to provide them with a substantial inheritance, with a particular desire to help them improve their own retirement scenario in the future.

Jim and Mary also wished they could do more for some charities they cared about, but they weren't sure they could without risking the retirement lifestyle they had earned or disinheriting their kids. They were also concerned that the growing national debt could lead to tax increases, so the Roth IRA opportunity intrigued them. Based on their own research and work with their current financial advisor, a conversion of Jim's IRA to a Roth IRA looked pretty good to them, even before they came in to meet with us. By converting the traditional IRA to a Roth IRA, paying the income taxes on the IRA balance now, and then allowing the funds to grow in the Roth IRA tax-deferred to eventually come out income tax-free, they estimated they would save almost $800,000 in income taxes over the next 30 years and provide about $300,000 more for their kids. But at the end of the day the numbers did not excite them, so they decided that it might not be worth the hassle. After all, they had a retirement to enjoy!

We were able to help by completing a more thorough and comprehensive planning process which included a financial analysis and simulation of a combination of integrated strategies that more fully accounted for their hopes and dreams as well as their risks and needs. We showed them a way to convert the IRA to a Roth IRA, enjoy an even higher level of retirement lifestyle than they had originally planned, generate significant tax deductions in the year of the IRA conversion, save $1,080,000 in income taxes over the next

30 years, give $1,600,000 more to their favorite charities, and provide $2,100,000 more for their children, part of which will be received as tax-free income over the children's lifetimes.

Jim and Mary's plan integrated an array of products, strategies, and structures. They invested in two differently designed annuities inside their new Roth IRA. By using annuities they leveraged the investments to provide a guaranteed death benefit inside one annuity for the portion that would pass to their children tax-free, and a guaranteed lifetime withdrawal benefit inside a second annuity for the portion that would supply lifetime income. They gifted the highly appreciated piece of investment real estate to a Charitable Remainder Trust (CRT), which allowed them to sell the real estate without any capital gains tax and reinvest the sale proceeds into a diversified investment portfolio to potentially grow the trust assets while providing them with additional lifetime income that is not fully taxable. After their deaths, the remaining assets in the trust will pass to their favorite charities, creating a larger, lasting legacy for the causes they want to impact. Their newfound higher annual income helped to increase their lifestyle, as they had secretly hoped, which allowed them to make several gifts to help with their grandchildren's education, and to fund an annual premium for a guaranteed life insurance contract, which would later serve to provide additional wealth to their family, replacing the value of the investment property donated to the Charitable Remainder Trust.

Bill—tax-free inheritance to son and a charitable legacy

Bill's wife, Betty, passed away 10 years ago. Since her death, he has become very involved in an international teacher training ministry through his local church, where he has personally found an outlet and means for coping with the loss of his wife. During a meeting with his attorney to update his will, he was made aware of the fact that his son would probably have to withdraw from his $6 million IRA to pay the estate taxes at Bill's death. This would cause the IRA not only to be subject to estate taxes, but the distribution to pay the estate tax would also be subject to income taxes. To avoid having a large portion of his IRA go to taxes, it was recommended to Bill to consider a traditional estate planning technique of purchasing a trust-owned life insurance policy to create liquidity for his son to pay the estate tax. At his death, the proceeds from the life insurance would cover the estate taxes, leaving the IRA intact for his son to draw on gradually over his lifetime.

Bill was casually discussing this situation with his pastor one day. The pastor suggested that he meet with us. We had been formally assisting the church with helping church members to better understand their capacity for planned gifts. The idea was to grow an endowment for the long-term support of the church's community outreach and international ministry work. When Bill first met with us, he was past the age of 70½, which compels him to take a required minimum amount of distributions from his IRA each year. He didn't particularly want the distributions or need it for income to support himself.

Therefore, we showed him how he could use his IRA required minimum distributions to fund life insurance in a trust, as his attorney had suggested. But, instead of using the insurance to pay the tax and preserve the IRA for his son, he could use the insurance policy to provide his son with a trust-owned guaranteed life insurance policy with a $7 million tax-free death benefit. By using the life insurance policy to provide an inheritance to his son, Bill can then name his church as the beneficiary of the IRA, which would create a lasting legacy with the church and avoid both estate and income taxes.

From Bill's perspective, this planning would accomplish both of his goals. The church's community outreach and international ministry endowment would stand to gain close to $6 million, and his son would receive a larger tax-free inheritance. Bill actually got emotional in our office when he completely grasped and understood his full potential. He expressed how he would have loved for his wife to have been there to share the joy he felt. The blessing extended to us, we assure you!

John and Diane—preserve family business with lasting philanthropy

John and Diane have worked hard to build their family business. All three of their adult children are active in the business, which, after years of toil and sacrifice, now produces a substantial and solid income for the entire family. John and Diane have been gradually gifting a few shares of stock in the business to their children each year, using the annual gift exclusion to each child to avoid gift taxes. However, their attorney and accountant both think that at its current rate of growth, the business will grow to such a value that is still likely to create significant estate taxes when the remaining shares pass to the kids at their death. The attorney and accountant suggested John and Diane utilize their lifetime exemptions to transfer more ownership of the business to their children and fund a trust-owned life insurance program to eventually pay the potential estate tax liability. This would protect the family from later having to sell shares in the business to raise cash for the payment of the estate tax.

John serves on the board of a local Boy Scouts council for which we were working as a resource to their individual and family donors. John is a passionate former Scout, Scout leader, and now board member. He considers the skills he learned in Scouting to be a foundation for his success in so many other areas of his life. You could say, as they like to say in the Boy Scouts, that John "bleeds khaki." John contacted us after learning that several of his fellow board members had benefited from consulting with us. We had been able to help them make an even greater impact on the Boy Scouts as a more significant part of their legacies.

We were able to show John and Diane how they could pass their business on to their family without incurring estate taxes and create a lasting legacy of philanthropy for their family. We did this by recommending that they add an irrevocable trust and a family-led charity, in their case, a Donor Advised Fund (DAF), to their estate plan. In so doing, they added a provision to leave an optimal percentage of their business to their DAF after their deaths. With our assistance, they would ultimately change the recipient of the annually gifted shares in the company from the kids directly to the new irrevocable trust, and then use the annual income distributions paid from the company to the trust to invest in an increased amount of life insurance. By rearranging the family's existing insurance and estate planning provisions, the family would then be in a position to use the insurance proceeds to purchase the business from the DAF after John and Diane's death, preserving the business within the family and at the same time completely avoiding the estate tax. Instead of a great asset like life insurance being used to fund government programs through an involuntary and unnecessary tax payment, the family would be allowed to do good, as they personally determine, through their DAF. We probably don't need to tell you, but they were delighted and excited with this result!

Discovering the resources

How do you find your place in this land of opportunity? Follow your heart and your head, and leverage outside resources for guidance. There are innumerable strategic gift planning tools available for your personal reflection. You can find many of the tools that we like best on our website (www. domorethatmatters.com).

For many of you, the question "What can I do?" might feel overwhelming because there is such a vast ocean of need out there. And because you may be coming to terms with your excess wealth for the first time, you may not have had the chance to think about the opportunity to live more and give more meaningfully and adequately. Tools, such as those we make available in this book, can help you to identify your areas of interest and passion, think about what results you'd like to help create in those areas, and then decide how to best go about making it happen. For some planned gifts, it may be wise to partner with an existing charitable organization, and for others you may consider starting your own family-led charity.

Community foundations can be another terrific resource for you to consider. These are independent philanthropic organizations in a specific geographical area. The foundations build permanent collections of endowment funds contributed from many donors to benefit various nonprofits in that area. We highly recommend that you check out your local community foundations.

Our sincere desire with this book is to get more people in the game of making a difference with their excess wealth— and to realize that it is about so much more than money. We pray that you will embrace this season of your life and celebrate just how valuable you could be. The choice about whether to take action and specifically what to do is all yours. For us—and for our clients—the rocking chair and "retiring" isn't an option. We all have gifts, talent, and passion that are too valuable not to share, so let's give it away!

"When you have a choice and don't make it, that in itself is a choice."

—**WILLIAM JAMES,** American philosopher and psychologist, 1842–1910

Chapter Eleven

ACTION: MAKE IT HAPPEN

The best-laid plans and goals will do nothing if they are not implemented. You may be fully in touch with how you want to help the world; you may be well past any worries that philanthropy will shortchange your family; and you may even understand just how much you can do. None of that matters unless you take action. For starters, write it down. Establish specific goals. Tell someone, or several someones. And then, just do it!

Team Hoyt

Perhaps you are familiar with the incredibly inspirational duo of Team Hoyt, the father-son pair who compete in grueling marathon, duathlon, and triathlon races. Rick was born in

1962 to Dick and Judy Hoyt. As a result of oxygen depriva-
tion to Rick's brain at the time of his birth, he was diagnosed
a spastic quadriplegic with cerebral palsy. Dick and Judy were
advised to institutionalize Rick because there was no chance
of his recovering to lead a "normal" life.

But nobody was going to tell this couple what was and
what was not possible for their son and for themselves. Dick
and Judy were determined to advocate for Rick's inclusion in
the community, sports, education, and the workplace. They
believe—and have rallied a legion of other believers who
agree—that all things are possible. Their motto is "Yes, You
Can!"

Team Hoyt's first competition was a local 5-mile benefit
run in 1977. Since then, they have competed in more than
1,000 races—with Dick running and pushing Rick in a special
racing chair. They have realized these amazing achievements
because of each other. They demonstrate a powerful example
of how love, desire, and passion, coupled with a commitment to each other and a higher purpose, can enable you to
do seriously difficult things—things most people tell us we
could never do.

Clearly, Rick would not have been able to accomplish
this on his own. Nor is it likely that his father would have
been motivated enough to have done this on his own either.
Behind the scenes of their public team, there certainly are
loved ones and other supporters who have helped them make
it happen.

But Team Hoyt didn't stop there. They recognized their
platform and the opportunity to lead and influence others

for good. They founded The Hoyt Foundation in 1989 as a nonprofit organization that aspires to build the individual character, confidence, and self-esteem of America's disabled young people through inclusion in all facets of daily life. The Hoyt Foundation also provides advice and support to groups and individuals who share this mission.

Each year, Team Hoyt's primary spokespeople—world-renowned athletes Dick and Rick Hoyt—speak before community and professional groups and participate in numerous road races and other endurance events. It is not hard to see what matters most to this family.

Team Hoyt is such a beautiful and vivid picture of the power of togetherness and the help it so clearly provides all of us in persisting, continuing to press on, and finishing our lives strong. We can set out with the best intentions, but real success will require pushing through the disappointments, disillusionments, and inevitable setbacks. Staying focused and allowing ourselves to be held accountable to our commitments and decisions can be invaluable.

We'd like to challenge you with the very real fact, all too often ignored, that you cannot do it on your own. And, even if you could, it is just a whole lot more fun to do it together. We believe that as human beings, we were made to live and make our impact on this world in community. We are better together.

Throughout history, the most effective leaders in any area of society have recognized that they need the gifts, skills, and expertise that others have, and so they have surrounded themselves with those people. As we reach out, it is uplifting to remember that our giving and how we choose to make a difference is also an opportunity for others to give. It is not just our lives and those we are serving who are touched and changed. Like Team Hoyt, you will not only accomplish your goals, but inspire others along the way.

We have all heard of the "six degrees of separation" concept: Anyone can be connected to others they don't know through six relationships tied to people they do know. With the help of today's technology, these connection points have become that much closer—in some situations, it is closer to three or four degrees of separation. With the ability of our teams and relationships, social media and other technologies, the opportunity to expand our horizons and the effectiveness of our work also becomes easier. One plus one can equal so much more than two.

Team (your name here)

You need a team. We seem to have made that point pretty clear, or at least we hope so. Typically, you would be well-served to have a team coordinator—your financial quarter-back, if you will—who will work to communicate your "go" signal to other members of the team. He or she will ensure that all of the parts of your plan are implemented and maintained, will serve as the primary conduit for important communication, and will help you achieve maximum impact.

When we talk about your impact, there are two scales of measurement—your life and your legacy. But perhaps even more telling as useful measures are your money and your purpose. You and your team should be continually assessing where you are. Is your purpose to serve your money, or is your money serving your purpose?

We meet with clients at least annually to review their goals and objectives. These are the objectives that they have written down, the ones of key importance for them to accomplish for themselves and their loved ones, and beyond. Each goal falls into one of those life or legacy categories; our dreams and "lifeprints" are a blend of both.

Increasingly, if the planning process has been comprehensive and successful, you should feel an ever-improving sense of peace, freedom, and impact. See our "Finishing Strong" diagram below, which can be a useful focusing and assessment tool.

Finishing Strong

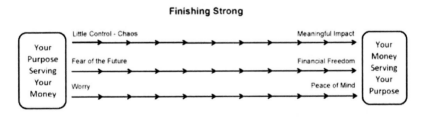

Where do you currently see yourself on each continuum?

Finishing Strong Takes Strategic Delegation
Not How? but <u>Who?</u>

The key to success, as with any great team, is strategic delegation. Leverage others with the expertise, skill, and relationships that you need but don't personally possess. Everyone needs to understand and perform his or her role and job. When it comes to life and legacy planning, the right financial professional can make all the difference in terms of helping you finish strong.

Is your purpose serving your money and running you ragged? Or are you living so that your money serves your purpose? Each of us is somewhere on a continuum between those extremes. And most everyone would like to be more intentional, more directive, and more purposeful with financial decisions.

Those who serve their money tend not to plan, allowing their financial life to unfold in front of them. As a result they tend to feel out of control, fear the future, and worry about the unknown. By contrast, we have observed three characteristics among people and families whose money is serving their purpose. They enjoy a heightened sense of sleep-at-night peace, walk-away freedom, and the feeling that they are making a meaningful impact.

Where would you put yourself on this continuum? Wherever you find yourself, how do you move to the right, toward the three characteristics of someone whose money is serving his or her purpose? The answer is not what you can do, but to whom you can strategically delegate this process. Who can show you how to move from a life of concern, fear and worry to a life of freedom, peace of mind, and meaningful impact? Just as in so many other areas of your life, if you have to accomplish something outside your realm of expertise, you should find a capable, skilled, and experienced resource.

The way to finish strong with your wealth is to begin moving intentionally toward creating the life and legacy of purpose that you desire. Start the right conversations and find and build a relationship of trust with the right professional.

Among the characteristics of the right professional are a proven track record, demonstrated expertise and results similar to those you want to create, and an intentional process. It is important that you demand a professional relationship with someone who relies upon and believes in systematic approaches to creating consistent results. The right process, person and firm will be able to bring the greatest value to what you are attempting to create through your personal impact and the ways in which you desire to make a difference with your excess wealth.

Monitoring and refining your plans

As the years pass, you should be continually re-evaluating the objectives that you have established. Outlooks change, usually subtly but sometimes radically, over time. That is why you must regularly work with your team to consider whether you are making the impact you intended. Are you hitting that bulls-eye? If you are not, where do you need to adjust your aim?

What do you need to change? Has anything been tripping you up or holding you back?

Sometimes it is your own cautious nature that may not be in touch with reality. A couple who were longtime clients recently came in for a financial review. One of their goals was to retire at age 65, and though the husband had recently retired, the wife was three years short of that. She looked exhausted. She was ready to retire—and a review of their finances indicated that she certainly could. The loss of three years of her income was really insignificant in the big picture.

But it took a few more meetings to get them to the point of realizing that. Finally, the husband, who had been reluctant, looked at his wife across the table and said, "You should do it, I know you can do it." Her face reflected a great sense of relief and excitement at the prospect. That is the sense of relief clients feel when they finally realize that they will be able to do what they had hoped financially. It is what begins to further release their spirit of generosity. They are finally able to begin looking outside themselves more than they ever had before.

In addition to monitoring your financial and estate planning, you also need to periodically review any specific philanthropic planning you have done to make sure the organizations you are supporting are staying true to their stated mission. Just as your own priorities can change, charities sometimes redefine their purpose or limit or expand their objectives. A charity that you once admired may fall out of your favor—either because it changed or because you changed your mind. You don't want to find yourself giving to a cause that you don't truly believe in. You may also find or be introduced to a new organization more in line with your passion and worthy of your support. It is important to maintain both oversight and flexibility.

However your philanthropic plan is designed, whatever specific goals you have, you want to be sure that you are hitting the bogeys, that you are making progress. Things in life will change. The tax code will change. Obstacles will arise in each of our lives—as will a wealth of opportunities. You want to be prepared to do the right thing.

Building momentum

In anything that you strive to accomplish, whether it is to get in shape, or learn a language, or acquire any new skill, you build momentum as you make progress. Success is inspiring. Philanthropy is like that, too. You start to see the impact you can have in the world, and when that starts to build momentum, you want to accomplish even more.

People start out with small steps and soon are making the strides that in time will significantly contribute to a better world. There is immense power, as we have seen, in the delicate flap of a butterfly's wings.

"What are you going to do with your one and only life?"

—BILL HYBELS, PASTOR, Willow Creek Community Church

Conclusion

WHAT ON EARTH AM I HERE FOR?

We all want our lives to matter, to count for something, to have a purpose. To accept this reality takes courage, humility, and honesty. You must ask yourself what your "why" is, and then seriously evaluate what is possible.

In 2002, Pastor Rick Warren, of Saddleback Church in Lake Forest, California, wrote the book *The Purpose Driven Life*. Since that time, the book has officially broken eight-digit sales, and its buyers have spanned nearly all faith backgrounds and beliefs, including atheists and agnostics. Why? Because people want to know—we all want to know—what on earth we are here for.

We can choose to accept this fact or ignore it. Our decision will either help us to further experience the person we have been uniquely created to be, or not. What we choose can make a world of difference, or not. Be honest with yourself: Once you are clear about your "why" and what you really care about, if you knew and really believed you could, wouldn't you? Of course you would!

You owe it to yourself, those you love, your community, and our world to take this seriously. Don't make the common mistake of assuming you know it all or that you are all set. From experience, we know all too well that sometimes we just don't know what we don't know. In law schools, one of the first things that students are taught is that "ignorance of the law is no excuse." The same can be said for your life and your legacy. You must figure it out. If not now, when?

More than they said they could

It was 2006, and Blake Mycoskie was visiting Argentina. He and his sister had been there as contestants in the CBS reality show "The Amazing Race"—they had placed third in the show's race in 2002—and he decided to revisit some of the areas that they had sprinted through during the competition. He wanted the true experience that one can achieve only by slowing down.

While traveling through the Argentinian villages, he noticed that many of the children in the grip of poverty lacked shoes. He saw the blisters and sores on young feet, leaving the kids at risk of infection and disease. In addition, he discovered that any child without shoes would not be able to attend school. Some families rotated a single pair of shoes between their children so that each would have the opportunity to attend school at least once a week.

Mycoskie found this unacceptable and considered setting up a nonprofit charitable organization, but he quickly dismissed the idea because the nonprofit would always depend on gifts. Instead, he looked for a better model—a form of capitalism that would be creative and redemptive. Then he learned how to make the indigenous canvas shoes.

Upon returning to the United States, he started a company, TOMS Shoes (which he devised from the phrase "Shoes for a Better Tomorrow"). TOMS has since sold many thousands of pairs of the canvas shoes in stores around the world and online. For each pair sold, a pair has been donated to a child in need. Shoes have been given to children in countries including Argentina, South Africa, Ethiopia, Rwanda, Guatemala, Haiti, and the United States.

Mycoskie has been an entrepreneur since college. He is a man who devoted his talents, energy, and financial capacity to an endeavor that he believed would make a difference in the world—and by which he, too, could profit. He observed a need and figured out how to make the most strategic impact with what was available to him. He took action.

"Be the change you want to see in the world," Gandhi said—a quote that is one of Mycoskie's favorites. Many people allow their lives to just happen. They strive to live by the golden rule, treating others fairly and generously. They pursue the American dream and do their best to enjoy life, but they just allow their lives to unfold without much thought about the lasting impact they could have on their family, community, and the world.

Today, the traditional idea of philanthropy is being expanded to include giving, serving, and acting for the common good through volunteer work and social action. For many of us with rich life experiences, marketplace skills, substantial capabilities, and relationships, this idea resonates.

Within this broader definition of philanthropy, there are countless examples of young people who have been inspired by others' examples or touched by a need they have observed, who then have taken action boldly to create solutions. One undeniable reality is that when we can couple our maturity, wisdom, and experience with the next generation's energy and creativity, the possibilities seem boundless.

There are kids like Zach Bonner, who collected bottled water for Hurricane Charlie victims in 2005, and then, at age 12, walked from Florida to Los Angeles to raise money in support of agencies serving homeless children and youth. Or young teens Brittany and Robbie Bergquist, who felt moved to help a U.S. soldier in Iraq pay his $8,000 cell phone bill and launched a national effort to recycle used cell phones and used the proceeds to buy millions of prepaid phone cards for troops stationed overseas.

Many of today's young and successful entrepreneurs—like Blake Mycoskie—have pioneered unique business models which show that meeting consumer demands and also addressing the needs of people around the globe are compatible and complementary goals. Others, like Facebook creator Mark Zuckerberg, have chosen with intention to live modestly and use their wealth to benefit charitable causes and nonprofit organizations.

Because it is so important for our lives to be positive role models to the next generation, we must demonstrate these philanthropic values in practical ways. Each time that people see us voluntarily offering our time, talent, and treasure to causes and organizations that matter to us, they get a chance to see a real-life example that they can appreciate and emulate. This can be an even more powerful and positive experience when our children and family members are able to participate with us.

These actions, what some call the law of reciprocity and others call "sowing and reaping," are real and active principles in all of our lives. If our end goals are big enough and sincere enough, these can fuel our "means" in amazing ways. As we give, we receive, and usually far more than we could have dreamed.

We hope that this book has encouraged you to become more engaged and in touch with your true potential and more committed to taking your plan, your life, and your legacy to the next level. Once you are committed to a cause, give it your utmost. If you are open to rethinking and reevaluating the wealth of your life, you may find that you have more financial capacity than you ever imagined.

If this book has opened your eyes to the possibilities, we have succeeded. We have helped you to begin releasing that music that is still locked up inside you. And ours is a world that is sorely in need of your song.

"Simplicity is the most deceitful mistress that ever betrayed man."

—HENRY B. ADAMS, American historian, 1838–1918

ADVANCED PLANNING

While we often recommend specific strategies for the advanced planning needs of our clients, some principles almost always hold true—such as the need to maximize control, build in flexibility, and improve tax efficiency.

Certainly, any good plan will minimize or eliminate estate taxes, if applicable, as well as reduce income taxes by applying the most current tax code provisions. One thing that many people don't realize, however, is that a zero federal estate-tax plan is actually possible and legal. And because they are unaware of this (having not planned holistically and comprehensively), they usually make mistakes that can reduce the amount available for themselves or their legacy and philanthropy.

Also, there are a variety of straightforward, well-accepted, tried-and-true strategies, products, and tactics that most people would be wise to consider within their plans. We'll share some of these in this appendix.

The power of leverage

Leverage is when an investment, insurance policy, or planning technique creates more wealth than was originally invested or put into the strategy. In using leverage within strategic financial planning, you can actually end up in many cases with exponentially more for the things you care about most. This especially applies to the use of tax strategies, legal structures, and financial products that you can leverage for a far greater financial impact. Some of these strategies have existed for close to a century.

The government realizes that healthy, vibrant nonprofits are in everyone's best interest and that their work will mean less of a toll on the governmental budgets. Nonprofits can typically do with a dollar what it could take the government four or five dollars to do. In an effort to encourage philanthropic giving, Congress created tax incentives and strategies for leaving wealth to charitable beneficiaries. These tax advantages have been in place for generations.

The U.S. government wants you to take charge of your giving. You are by no means cheating on your taxes when you leverage and take advantage of "breaks" and incentives in the tax code and financial marketplace. You can better facilitate the flow of money to charitable, community, and civic purposes. It is smart and savvy tax planning, not illegal tax evasion.

Tax strategies you should know about

ROTH IRA CONVERSIONS

At the time of publishing of this book, the rules governing Roth IRA conversions provide that there is no longer an income limitation dictating who may convert a traditional IRA to a Roth IRA (at least for the time being). The advantage being that once you convert the traditional IRA to a Roth IRA, you pay the income tax on the traditional IRA at the time of the conversion and then it grows tax-deferred. All of the growth, income, and originally converted amount eventually comes out of the Roth IRA income-tax free to you or your beneficiaries.

Financial professionals often oversimplify the analysis supporting this decision. For most advisors, it has basically become a zero-sum game looking at which point in time you will be in a lower income-tax bracket: Will it be now when you plan to do your conversion, or later in retirement? When do you plan to take the money out to supplement your income? If your personal tax rate and timing of taking income distributions are the only two relevant comparison points in your situation, then we would tend to agree that a simple calculation is probably the right level of inquiry.

However, many of the clients we serve don't need this money, now or ever. In fact, they most often work to delay taking any money out of retirement accounts for as long as they legally can. They don't need additional income from the accounts and want to continue the tax deferral. And truth be told, if they could, they would just let the accounts grow, tax-deferred, until their dying day. For most of these folks, these accounts are earmarked for their family or their charitable legacy.

This dramatically changes the type of inquiry, as compared with the traditional analysis of most advisors that we shared at the outset. The reason is that when we leave a child or grandchild a Roth IRA, they are able to continue to stretch out the tax deferral period for the remainder of their life expectancy, income tax free! The financial projections of the wealth that can be created, through this sort of amazing pension-like inheritance, can sometimes be almost overwhelming. The only problem with this terrific and valuable strategy is the hurdle of paying the income tax on the traditional IRA or retirement account when you make the conversion to the Roth IRA. However, incorporating the establishment of a lasting, charitable legacy at the same time as the conversion can greatly reduce the tax consequences while establishing the Roth IRA's tax-free wealth transfer to future generations.

FAMILY-LED CHARITY

Charitable Remainder Trusts (CRTs) allow a highly appreciated asset to be "gifted" into the trust, subsequently sold without immediately incurring any capital gains tax and then reinvested as appropriate. Income then begins being paid out to you and usually your spouse for your lifetimes. Then, any remaining assets still in the trust at the death of the surviving spouse would pass on to your named charitable beneficiaries. This type of trust provides you with an immediate income tax deduction. Because this trust will pay you income for life, it is referred to as a split-interest trust. The two interests are your lifetime income interest and the charitable beneficiaries' remainder interest. Due to the split-interest nature of the trust, the deductions it creates are usually lower than an outright gift to a public charity. But, keep in mind, an outright gift to a public charity doesn't pay you an income for life. So, it really depends on what you need within your plan.

CRTs have become very popular, but not nearly as much as Donor Advised Funds (DAFs). The DAF is offered and administered by a registered public charity, so any assets you gift to this type of fund will qualify for the full level of available tax deduction, just as if you were giving it to the United Way or any other charity or nonprofit. With a DAF, the major difference is that you are able to "advise" about how you'd like the money invested and to what organizations you'd prefer it ultimately be donated. While you exercise considerable influence as the donor adviser in conjunction with the DAF, the DAF's board actually has legal control of the funds. In fact, many DAF organizations sign agreements with the IRS making it completely clear that the donor does not have legal control of the funds. It is customary, of course, for a board to honor the wishes of the donor. However, for some people, this lack of legal control prompts them to establish a private foundation instead. Distributions do not need to be in the same year as the contributions. The DAF can continue for your lifetime and can pass on to future generations to administer. The tax deductibility of the contributions may be limited, but excess charitable deductions can carry forward.

These popular vehicles are available through financial firms like Fidelity, Schwab, and Vanguard, as well as through many community foundations, and certain large charitable organizations, such as National Christian Foundation and Jewish National Fund. We recommend consulting a tax advisor before initiating any philanthropic or charitable planning.

The CRT and DAF tax strategies, when used as part of an integrated plan design, are two powerful examples of ways to both leverage your wealth and reduce or eliminate taxes in favor of your family and charity. You may want to consider a Roth IRA conversion while also simultaneously making a strategic gift to one of these types of vehicles, thus creating some degree of offsetting income tax deductions. What if you could reduce or eliminate completely the federal income tax resulting from your otherwise substantially taxable Roth IRA conversion? Through this approach you can create a win-win result for your family and for charity, which is a pretty exciting possibility. We covered a real life situation demonstrating this integrated strategy back in chapter 10.

OTHER LEGAL STRUCTURES OF INTEREST

Section 509 of the Internal Revenue Code provides for the creation of private foundations. This is certainly something you may want to consider, but realize that these do come with reduced deductibility and greater oversight by the Internal Revenue Service. If you have a sufficient amount of wealth that you'd like to earmark for philanthropy and can envision a family extension of your philanthropy as something you'd like to be able to develop, a private or family foundation can be a wonderful way of making an impact and leaving a legacy by having it continue on after you have passed away. We often recommend considering an administration company like Foundation Source to assist with the compliance and with the various regulations that apply and keep it on solid ground long-term with the work you are endeavoring to accomplish.

The 509(a)(3) supporting organization (SO) is lesser known, but it is sometimes quite a powerful option and is just one level down from a full-fledged private foundation. This is an organization that effectively "piggy backs" onto a public charity. As such, the deductibility of gifts made to a SO are the same as they would be to a public charity, and since the regulators are operating at the public charity level, there is very little additional scrutiny at the SO level. The one caveat is that there really needs to be a legitimate synergy between the supported organization and the supporting organization. Governance needs to also be carefully patched together in a thoughtful manner. These can be very effective mechanisms to connect an outreach, civic, or even international work to a church or other faith tradition, while being able to also create an independent brand, entity, and identity in the marketplace.

The low-profit limited liability company, commonly referred to as the L3C, is a sort of hybrid nonprofit and for-profit organization. This is a really interesting and increasingly popular entity. The oldest statute in the United States that allows for these entities is in Vermont. There are close to 10 states or jurisdictions now recognizing these types of entities. The regulations must be carefully understood and complied with, and individual charitable contributions to these entities are not deductible. However, they are eligible for contributions by way of grants from foundations, so long as there can be established a "program related investment." Consult with an expert if you would like to explore this idea. If you have the right mix of wanting to have some level of profit permissible, have a legitimate social purpose, and like the idea of having foundations available as a nontraditional source of capital, these could be of interest to you.

There are a host of social venture capital firms popping up throughout the marketplace. These firms effectively take an approach similar to private equity firms in the for-profit marketplace, doing a heightened level of due diligence and regular monitoring beyond what the average philanthropist is capable of based on experience and available resources. While many of our clients want to give, they only want to give to something that they believe can work and make its intended impact. Aligning with these firms that truly evaluate and "invest" in causes and often assist charitable organizations that they believe will succeed is an excellent way to increase the odds of your success in pursuing your own legacy and philanthropic goals.

We highly recommend considering at least one of these relationships within your overall mix of philanthropic pursuits. Do your homework or reach out to us and we can provide you some guidance in this area. You can reach us through our website: www.domorethatmatters.com.

Maintaining excellence

Your philanthropic planning should be flexible enough to create the maximum benefit and allow for changes in your focus and priorities, which can evolve in unexpected ways. Build whatever you build to last, just as you would your own family and your own business. Carefully craft a mission statement, form a strategic advisory board, and even plan for succession issues. If you sincerely desire to maximize your unique impact on this world, you must treat this initiative with the same seriousness, professionalism, and sophistication as your most successful venture.

Whether your philanthropy is big or small, just starting or rising to the next level, we challenge you to have as an overarching goal: to sustain, preserve, protect, and pass on your values, purpose, and impact. Nobody else has been made uniquely like you. Your heart and your passion have the power to improve the world, and that can be one of your life's greatest blessings—if you discover it. Please consider going after it and doing something more that matters.

These are only a few of the various strategies and tactics available to individuals and families. For additional information and resources on advanced planning, visit our website, www.domorethatmatters.com.

RON WARE is an attorney and a financial planner. He is also the founder and president of Wealth Impact Partners and cofounder of the Do More That Matters Foundation. For over 20 years, Ron and his team have helped successful individuals and families discover and act upon their true financial capacity and personal passion to improve their impact with their wealth.

Ron holds himself out professionally as a personal legacy advisor. He believes that the central focus of "next level" financial and estate planning should be the life we have always wanted and the legacy by which we hope one day to be remembered. To Ron, this approach is what makes Wealth Impact Partners different. It is something distinctly more positive, and also more motivating, for the individuals and families he advises.

Through his *ActivateLegacy* program, Ron also has served as a valuable resource to charities and nonprofits and the people who care about them, by helping them better evaluate how they might be able to make major and planned gifts. Ron serves as an objective, expert resource to these individuals and families, as they earnestly explore approaches that could allow them to do more philanthropically.

Ron has an eye for design, and he often likens how his firm works with people to that of design-build architecture firms that help people design and then build more complete plans. He is a sought-after speaker as well as a gifted and passionate teacher. Two of Ron's most requested talks are: "Enhancing the Wealth of Your Life" and "So Much Purpose, So Little Time." He teaches regularly on behalf of an array of collaborative partners, including charitable organizations, faith-based groups, and other financial professionals. He also has had the rare honor and privilege of delivering an occasional Sunday sermon at his church.

Ron earned a juris doctor from Regent University in Virginia and a bachelor of science in business administration from Bryant University in Rhode Island. He is a lifelong entrepreneur and has been part of closely held family businesses since childhood.

"I firmly believe I'm here for a reason, just like all of us," Ron says. "I'm just one of the lucky ones who has found my one thing that I've been uniquely called to do—encouraging, empowering, and equipping others to experience more and do more with what they have. I consider it a huge blessing to have this opportunity to live out my values, and I'm privileged to help smart and successful people live out theirs."

Wealth Impact Partners
34 Washington St., Suite 205
Wellesley Hills, MA 02481
781.489.9805
ron@wealthimpactpartners.com
www.wealthimpactpartners.com

GREG HAMMOND guides successful families and business owners toward smarter decisions about their wealth in today's uncertain political, economic and social environment.

Greg is president of Hammond Iles Wealth Advisors and cofounder of the Do More That Matters Foundation. As a Wealth Impact Strategist for life and legacy, he is dedicated to helping people transform their financial picture into an organized, unified plan for their lifetimes and beyond. Greg has been in financial services for over 20 years and has clients in 30 states. He specializes in investment strategies and charitable planning for transfer of wealth between generations, legacy building, and protecting the value of an estate. He seeks to make the wealth transfer process a productive and meaningful experience by understanding a family's unique dynamics and values, educating family members about money management, and acting as a neutral facilitator.

Through shared life experiences and engaging humor, Greg brings the concept of superior planning alive with creativity, vitality and spontaneity as he delivers keynote presentations at conferences, estate-planning councils, churches and organizations. He moves people from passive listeners to active participants, empowering them to "do more that matters."

A graduate of Miami University in Oxford, Ohio, with a bachelor of science in accountancy, Greg began his career with a regional CPA firm. "When my first daughter was born," he says, "I took a look at the things that were important in life"—and among them was a desire to do more to help people than just prepare their taxes.

Transitioning to wealth management, he and his business partner, Scott Iles, eventually acquired the private practice where they worked in order to focus on helping people align their financial goals, life visions, risk tolerance, and philosophy so they can support their families and the causes they care about while preserving investments and generating income and estate tax benefits.

With a passion for the nonprofit organizations that enrich our world, Greg and Scott founded Planned Giving Strategies (PGS) in 2008. PGS consults with nonprofit organizations and educational institutions on planned giving program efficiency and related investing. On behalf of these organizations, Greg facilitates presentations that inspire, educate, and empower donors to create a thoughtfully planned charitable giving strategy with the potential to create income for a lifetime, give more to their heirs, and build their legacy.

"My father showed me through his actions and example that it's important to give back to the community, beyond supporting one's family," Greg says. "I feel, through my faith, that I'm called to do more. Each of us is blessed with unique gifts. My profession allows me to leverage knowledge and experience to help others and make a tremendous impact in the world. That's what motivates me."

Hammond Iles Wealth Advisors
100 Great Meadow Road, Suite 103
Wethersfield, CT 06109
800.416.1655
info@hammondiles.com
www.hammondiles.com

Greg Hammond and Ron Ware

Visit **www.domorethatmatters.com**
to access the resources mentioned in this book,
plus bonus content you can use to live more and give more.

A portion of the proceeds from the sale of this book will be directed to the **Do More That Matters Foundation Fund**. Created by co-authors Greg Hammond and Ron Ware, the foundation supports organizations and initiatives that seek to improve the lives of children and families through sustainable methods. Areas of domestic and international focus include: leadership development, economic development, health and wellness, and education.

CPSIA information can be obtained at www.ICGtesting.com
Printed in the USA
BVOW03s0747021013

332680BV00010B/64/P